Ann Greening
Mother of Edward Elgar

Dedicated to the memory of Margaret & Catherine Elgar,
& Brenda Watson, who died after this book was completed.

Ann Greening
Mother of Edward Elgar

Hilary Elgar, Brenda Watson & Michael Trott

BREWIN BOOKS

BREWIN BOOKS
19 Enfield Ind. Estate,
Redditch,
Worcestershire,
B97 6BY
www.brewinbooks.com

Published by Brewin Books 2024

© Hilary Elgar, Brenda Watson & Michael Trott, 2024

The authors have asserted their rights in accordance with the Copyright, Designs and Patents Act 1988 to be identified as the authors of this work.

All rights reserved. No part of this publication may be reproduced, stored in a retrieval system, or transmitted in any form or by any means, electronic, mechanical, photocopying, recording or otherwise, without the prior permission in writing of the publisher and the copyright owners, or as expressly permitted by law, or under terms agreed with the appropriate reprographics rights organisation. Enquiries concerning reproduction outside the terms stated here should be sent to the publishers at the UK address printed on this page.

The publisher makes no representation, express or implied, with regard to the accuracy of the information contained in this book and cannot accept any legal responsibility for any errors or omissions that may be made.

A CIP catalogue record for this book is available from the British Library.

ISBN: 978-1-85858-768-4

Printed and bound in Great Britain
by Hobbs The Printers Ltd.

Contents

List of Illustrations	vi
Foreword	viii
Preface	ix
Acknowledgements	xi

Part I: Ann's Story

1.	Greenings & Apperleys	3
2.	Ann's Childhood in Herefordshire, 1822-c.1840	21
3.	Ann's Youth & Early Adulthood, c.1840-1848	26
4.	Marriage & Family Life, 1848-1863	36
5.	Life at 10 High Street, 1863-1878 (first 15 years)	46
6.	Later Years in Worcester, 1878-1902	70
7.	Ann's Influence on Edward	89

Part II: Source Material

8.	Lucy's 'Reflections'	101
9.	Ann's Scrapbooks	108
10.	'Worcester Papers'	118

Part III: Background Information

11.	The Place of Women in Victorian Society	123
12.	Concern for Schooling in the Pre-Victorian Period	124
13.	The American Connection – Nineteenth-century Emigration	127
14.	Chronology	131
15.	Sources & Bibliography	133
16.	Notes	135
	Appendix: Extracts from 'Worcester Papers'	139
	Index	149

Boxes

A	(Chapter 1): The Spelling of Ann's Name and her Date of Birth	13
B	(Chapter 5): The Piano in Victorian Society	51
C	(Chapter 5): Worcester, A Lively City	52
D	(Chapter 5): The Popularity of Longfellow in Victorian Society	64
E	(Chapter 7): Similarities between the Upbringing of Elgar and Hardy	97
F	(Chapter 13): Extracts from John Greening's Journal	130

List of Illustrations

1. Map showing villages around Elmore and Westbury-on-Severn, Gloucestershire.
2. Portrait of Joseph Greening, Ann's father.
3. Greening graves at St John the Baptist's Church, Elmore, Gloucestershire.
4. Greening family tree.
5. Zechariah & daughter Mary Greening's graves at St John the Baptist's Church, Elmore, Gloucestershire.
6. Portrait of Esther Greening (née Apperley), Ann's mother.
7. Apperley family tree.
8. Tripod table made by wheelwright John Apperley and given to his daughter Esther (Ann's mother) on her marriage to Joseph Greening in 1806.
9. Note by Ann Greening under her grandfather's table.
10. Johannes Kip's 1712 engraving of Westbury-on-Severn, showing the church, the original late Elizabethan *Westbury Court* and *Westbury Court Garden*.
11. The Church of St Mary, St Peter & St Paul, Westbury-on-Severn, where Ann's parents married in 1806.
12. 1822 portrait of Hannah More by Henry William Pickersgill.
13. Map showing the districts around Weston-under-Penyard, Herefordshire.
14. Grave of Ann's parents, Joseph & Esther Greening, Claines Churchyard, Worcester.
15. *Handley*, Ann's childhood home near Pontshill, Herefordshire, in 1928.
16. *Handley* in 2021, with May Hill in the distance and the wooded Lea Bailey enclosure to the right.
17. Weston-under-Penyard from *Handley*.
18. Sampler of 1833 by Ann Greening.
19. Part of Charles Crisp's 1832 'Plan of the City of Worcester'.
20. The former *Shades Tavern*, 16 Mealcheapen Street, Worcester.
21. St John the Baptist's Church, Claines, Worcester.
22. *Nucketts Farm* (now *Blossom Farm*), Chatley, the Greenings' first home in Worcestershire.
23. William Elgar's 1845 map, showing directions from Worcester to *Nucketts Farm*, Chatley.

24. William Elgar, aged about 35 (1856).
25. *Ann at the Shades Tavern*, Worcester, by Tom Elgar.
26. Photograph of Ann, aged about 26 at the time of her marriage (1848).
27. Crayon drawing of 1856 by John C. Buckler of the Elgars' cottage at Broadheath (*The Firs*), Worcester, just before Edward was born there.
28. Photograph of Ann with Edward, 1859.
29. The Elgar Brothers music shop at 10 High Street, Worcester, c.1910.
30. The cathedral end of High Street, Worcester, c.1860.
31. Abbreviated Elgar family tree (two generations).
32. Cross-staves design on 'BACH' by Edward Elgar, 1866.
33. Photograph of Ann, c.1870.
34. Photograph of the Elgar children, 1868 (back row Edward & Pollie, front row Dot, Frank & Lucy).
35. Photograph by Vanderweyde of Edward Elgar at 21.
36. Facsimile of letter (page 1) from Ann to her granddaughter Carice on 5 March 1897.
37. Facsimile of letter (page 2) from Ann to her granddaughter Carice on 5 March 1897.
38. Photograph of Ann & William Elgar, c.1900.
39. Elgar family grave (including Ann), Astwood Cemetery, Worcester.
40. Sketch by Ann of St Mary's Church, Arlingham, near Gloucester, dated 22 May 1882.
41. A page from Ann's scrapbook (1).
42. A page from Ann's scrapbook (2).
43. A page from Ann's scrapbook (3).
44. A page from Ann's scrapbook (4).
45. Map of Wisconsin, U.S.A., showing John Greening's adopted town of Mazomanie.
46. Charles Greening, one of Ann's American nephews, who came to Worcester in 1900 to visit Ann.
47. Front page of 'Worcester Papers', 14 August 1852.
48. Front page of 'Worcester Papers', 4 September 1852.

Foreword

When we first began researching into Ann's life we were concerned that there would be insufficient interesting information for a book. How wrong we were! Despite our initial misgivings we have been able to piece together a life both surprising and significant.

Much of what we write is conjecture but based, so far as is possible, on solid historical evidence. What is certain is that Ann was a remarkable woman and perfect mother for Edward. She was a crucial focus inspiring his development, a fact he acknowledged publicly in Worcester Guildhall after her death.

Preface

In this age of the cult of celebrity it is easy to forget that all individuals are part of a huge network of influences. Even a genius is dependent on the support of many others. One of the most profound influences on Edward Elgar was someone who was not particularly musical, his mother, Ann. Little seemed to be known about her, yet she was his earliest and perhaps deepest source of inspiration.

The composer's great-niece Hilary Elgar has long felt that Ann's role in the development of his genius has been undervalued. This book, researched with Brenda Watson and Michael Trott, seeks to throw light on the kind of person she was and the innumerable ways in which she encouraged and inspired Edward.

We live today in an age when social justice, equality of treatment for all, freedom to think and develop as individuals, the possibility of overcoming barriers of poverty, low social status, lack of education, etc., are regarded as part of a humane society. Our story is about a woman born into a very different world. She was of low social status, grew up in an isolated rural situation, without formal opportunities for education and unsupported by any high-ranking person in society. Nevertheless, she came to fulfil an extraordinarily important role as a major influence on the life of perhaps England's greatest composer.

Comparison with Mary Arden, the mother of William Shakespeare, sheds some light on Ann's achievement. There are parallels. Both women were the daughters of farmers and Roman Catholic (Ann was a convert in adulthood). It is suspected that Mary was literate and had benefited from some education, and so it has been conjectured that she may well have fired William's imagination by story-telling as Ann clearly did with Edward. Mary would have been expected to support her husband in his business and run their household, much as Ann was three centuries later. There was gradually increasing social mobility in both Tudor and Victorian times in spite of rigid social distinctions. Outstanding artistic success was one way to rise socially which applied, of course, to both William Shakespeare and Edward Elgar.

What we do have regarding Ann Greening is historical evidence strongly suggesting the influence she had on her son. There are three main sources for this:

- the family journal 'Worcester Papers', in which Ann wrote about contemporary issues, thus revealing much about her attitude to life;

- her two scrapbooks of considerable length, which show clearly what interested her and that have many comments, some in her own handwriting, that indicate the type of character and values she regarded as important; and
- the memoir written by her eldest daughter, Lucy, in which much intimate detail is shared and we can occasionally almost hear Ann's voice.

Our story of Ann is, therefore, not just conjecture but rests on material which is available today for study by anyone interested to know why we say what we do about her. Of course, we wish we had more information to portray her life more fully but we think there is enough to show what an unusual person she was and how, despite so many drawbacks, she achieved something profound – the nurturing of a genius.

We invite readers to make their own assessment. We see Ann as a woman who unselfconsciously broke through many barriers, whose open-minded and vivacious interest in life was infectious to those around her, and who, through the son she inspired, made a huge contribution to the cultural life of Britain today. It is a story of social mobility, of a woman transcending the claustrophobic limits of class and affluence, who knew what she stood for and pursued it with integrity, modesty and charm, free of any aggressive awareness of victim-status.

She achieved what she did through living life simply, courageously and with humour, far removed from today's promotion of victim-mentality.

Acknowledgements

The authors wish to thank Kevin Allen, Dr Elizabeth Ashton, Chris Bennett, Richard Smith, Emeritus Professor John Whenham and Jean Yates for their generous assistance in the preparation of this book. In particular, thanks are due to the following for permission to reproduce illustrations.

Chris Bennett:
8. Tripod table made by wheelwright John Apperley.
9. Note by Ann Greening under her grandfather's table.
18. Sampler of 1833 by Ann Greening.

The Elgar Foundation:
2. Portrait of Joseph Greening, Ann's father.
6. Portrait of Esther Greening (née Apperley), Ann's mother.
23. William Elgar's 1845 map, showing directions from Worcester to *Nucketts Farm.*
24. William Elgar, aged about 35 (1856).
25. *Ann at the Shades Tavern, Worcester*, by Tom Elgar.
26. Photograph of Ann, aged about 26 at the time of her marriage (1848).
27. Crayon drawing of 1856 by John C. Buckler of the Elgars' cottage at Broadheath.
28. Photograph of Ann with Edward, 1859.
29. The Elgar Brothers' music shop at 10 High Street, Worcester, c.1910.
32. Cross-staves design on 'BACH' by Edward Elgar, 1866.
33. Photograph of Ann, c.1870.
34. Photograph of the Elgar children, 1868.
35. Photograph by Vanderweyde of Edward Elgar at 21.
36-37. Facsimile of letter from Ann to her granddaughter Carice.
38. Photograph of Ann & William Elgar, c.1900.
40. Sketch by Ann of St Mary's Church, Arlingham.
41-44. Pages from Ann's scrapbook.
47. Front page of 'Worcester Papers', 14 August 1852.
48. Front page of 'Worcester Papers', 4 September 1852.

Mary Hughes:
5.   Zechariah & daughter Mary Greening's graves at St John the Baptist's Church, Elmore.

The National Portrait Gallery:
12.   1822 portrait of Hannah More by Henry William Pickersgill.

Richard Smith:
14.   Grave of Ann's parents, Joseph & Esther Greening, Claines Churchyard, Worcester.
46.   Charles Greening, one of Ann's American nephews.

Robin Trott:
11.   The Church of St Mary, St Peter & St Paul, Westbury-on-Severn.

Richard Watts:
15.   Handley, Ann's childhood home near Pontshill, Herefordshire, in 1928.

Worcestershire Archive & Archaeology Service:
19.   Charles Crisp's 1832 'Plan of the City of Worcester'.

Sam Eedle Design drew the maps (Illust. 1, 13 & 45).

Part I

Ann's Story

1.
Greenings & Apperleys

Ann's father, Joseph Greening
William Langland began his famous allegorical poem *Piers Plowman*: 'And one morning in May on the Malvern Hills I witnessed a wonder which I warrant was magic.'[1] In a similar way to the poet writing in the fourteenth century, both Ann Greening and her son Edward Elgar were inspired – indeed overwhelmed – by the wonderful scenery around Malvern.

Ann was staying with a friend in Colwall, a village near Malvern, from which there is an excellent view of the Iron Age hill fort known as The British Camp. Edward visited her and, as they admired the view, Ann said:

> *'Oh Ed! Look at the lovely old hill, can't we write some tale about it?' 'Do it yourself, Mother.' He held my hand with a firm grip. 'Do,' he said. 'No, I can't, my day is gone if ever I could,' and so we parted – and in less than a month he told me Caractacus was all cut and dried and he had begun to work at it.*[2]

* * *

The Forest of Dean seems to us to be a somewhat forbidding and lonely part of Gloucestershire, large areas of which remain today probably much as they were in the early-nineteenth century when Ann was born there. Her father, Joseph, was a member of the large Greening family who farmed in Gloucestershire around the Severnside villages south of Gloucester (Illust. 1). This whole area was associated with the Greenings for generations, the earliest recorded being John Greening, who was farming in the village of Awre in 1493.

Joseph Greening (Illust. 2) was born in Elmore in 1780, the son of William and Martha Greening. The Church of St John the Baptist, where he was baptised, today lies hidden away among trees along a quiet road dotted with fine houses, one mile from the main part of the village (Illust. 3). Joseph died in 1848, when Ann was in her mid-twenties. (See Greening family tree, Illust. 4.)

The visitor today would find at least three Greening tombs in the churchyard at Elmore, including that of Zechariah, Ann's great-uncle, and his daughter Mary.[3] The headstones (Illust. 5) carry two poems; Zechariah lived to the ripe age of 87 yet had his gloomy moments as we can see:

*Afflictions sore, long time I bore.
All human health was vain
Till God did please, death should me seize
And ease me of my pain.*

His wife, Jane, died seven years later at the age of 84. Her poem has a more theological but equally austere theme:

*Engrave no flattery on my stone.
Man is by nature lost.
Salvation is by Christ alone.
Of what have we to boast?*

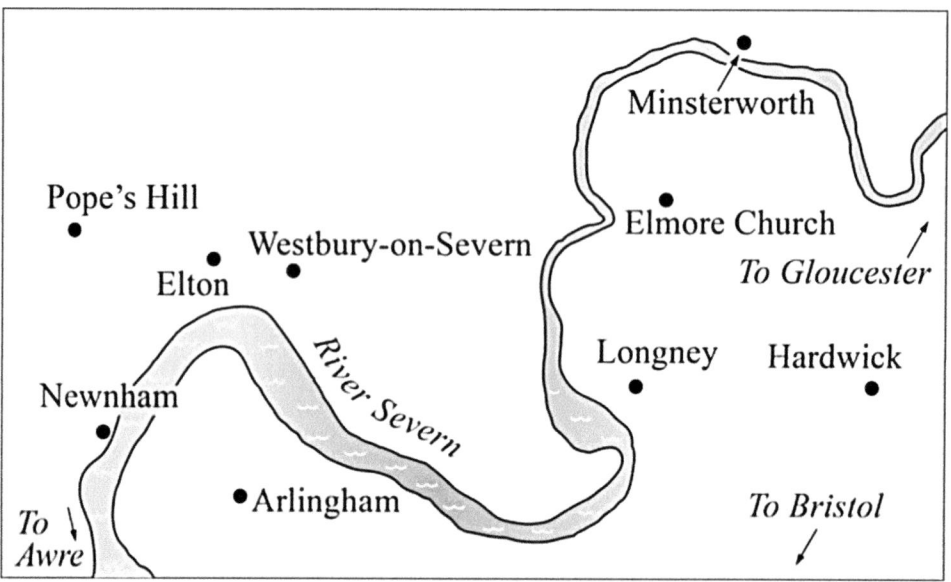

1. Map showing villages around Elmore and Westbury-on-Severn, Gloucestershire.

1. Greenings & Apperleys

2. Portrait of Joseph Greening, Ann's father.

3. Greening graves at St John the Baptist's Church, Elmore, Gloucestershire.

Ann's mother, Esther Apperley

Esther (or Hester) Apperl(e)y (Illust. 6) was born in the village of Elton-by-Newnham in 1784, the daughter of John and Anne Apperley. (See Apperley family tree, Illust. 7.) Her father was a wheelwright, who owned or worked on land at Pope's Hill, not far away. We know this because he gave his daughter Esther a wedding present of a tripod table he had made (Illust. 8).[4] In those candlelit days such a table was often used for placing candles. It survives at Elgar's Birthplace, and pasted to its underside is the following note (Illust. 9):

> *This table was made by William Apperly of Elton by Newnham, wheelwright – and given to his second daughter, Esther, on her marriage to Joseph Greening, May 26th 1806, at Westbury on Severn, Gloucestershire. From a tree grown on his own land at Popes Hill.*

* * *

Anne (sic) Elgar July 22nd 1882
his granddaughter

1. Greenings & Apperleys

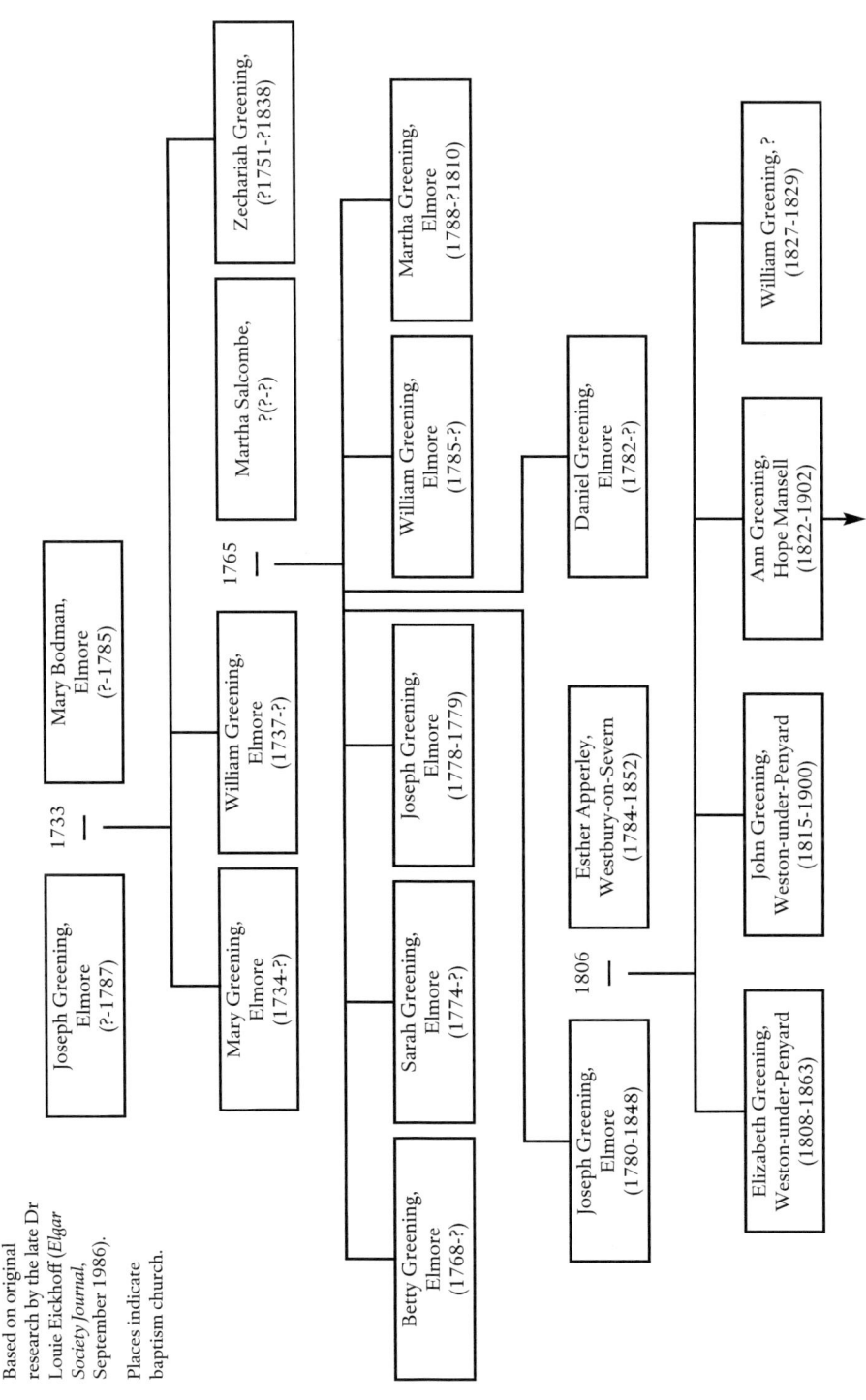

4. *Greening family tree.*

5. *Zechariah & daughter Mary Greening's graves at St John the Baptist's Church, Elmore, Gloucestershire.*

Wheelwrights were the 'craftsmen of the countryside'[5] and, given the complexity of cartwheel construction, making a small table was probably straightforward for John Apperley. In fact, as factory-made vehicles superseded wooden horse-drawn carts, many wheelwrights went into the furniture industry. This tripod table probably saw well over a century of service in the Greening and Elgar households.

Ann's parents were probably relatively poor, so would have had to work hard to provide for quite a numerous family. They clearly lived simple lives, self-sufficient, strong members of a community. Esther was certainly literate and probably really enjoyed reading as wide a range of reading matter as she was able to get hold of. They appear to have been intelligent but not necessarily at all well educated. Her father certainly was illiterate, as we know from the evidence of his marriage certificate on which he placed his thumb. Their lives would have been bounded by the agricultural cycle and parish activities associated with the church. Moreover, from the tombstones of Ann's aunt, Uncle John and Great-Uncle Zechariah, they were probably a devout family.

1. Greenings & Apperleys

6. *Portrait of Esther Greening (née Apperley), Ann's mother.*

Ann Greening: Mother of Edward Elgar

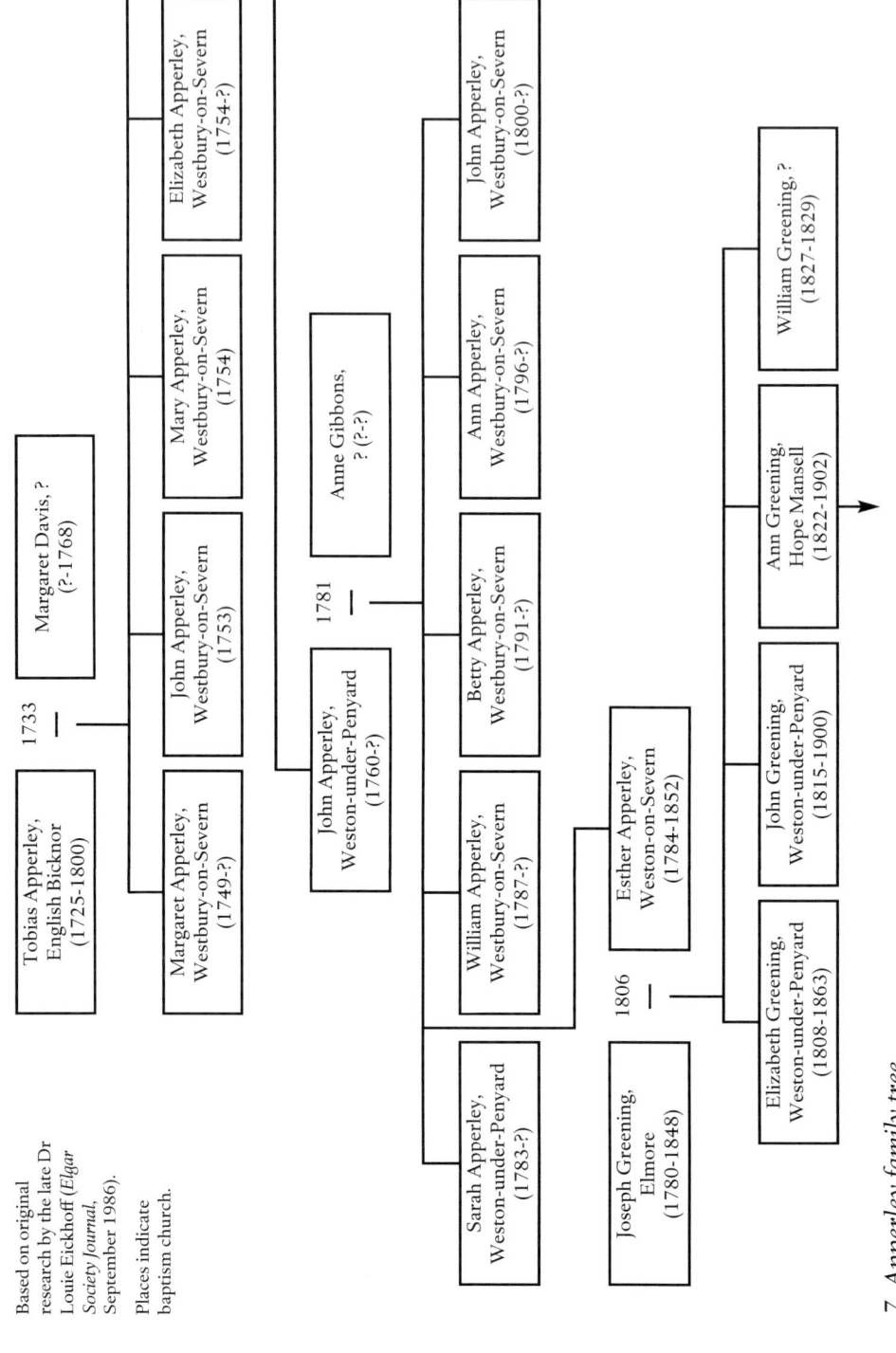

7. *Apperley family tree.*

1. Greenings & Apperleys

8. *Tripod table made by wheelwright John Apperley and given to his daughter Esther (Ann's mother) on her marriage to Joseph Greening in 1806.*

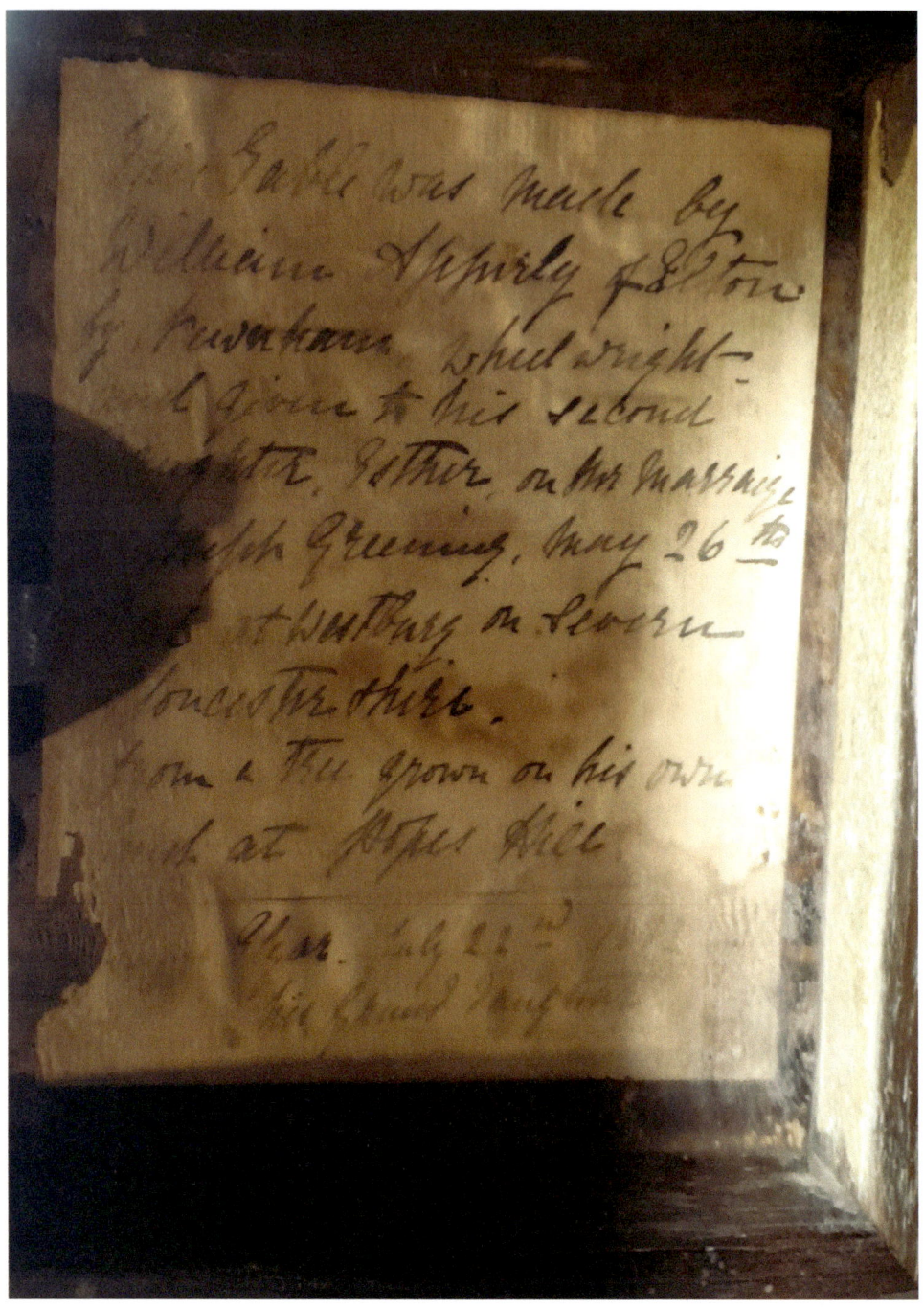

9. *Note by Ann Greening under her grandfather's table.*

Box A: The Spelling of Ann's Name and her Date of Birth

There is some confusion in the Elgar bibliography: some noted writers have used both 'Ann' and 'Anne'. However, the name on her mourning card and on the original kerbing around her grave at Astwood Cemetery in Worcester was 'Ann', and the authors take this as definitive. *The Elgars of Worcester* by K. E. L. and Marion Simmons (The Elgar Society, 1984) states in the notes (p.21) that Ann spelled her name without an 'e', but her husband, William, wrote 'Anne' at times: this is probably the source of confusion. Basil Maine consulted Elgar for his 1933 biography (*Elgar: His Life & Works*, 1933), in which Maine refers to 'Ann', and it is unlikely that Elgar would not have read the draft and drawn a misspelling of his mother's name to Maine's attention. Robert Buckley's 1905 biography of Elgar (*Sir Edward Elgar*, 1905) also refers to 'Ann', and Ann herself has sewn her name as 'Ann' on her sampler of 1833.

We are sure that Ann died on 1 September 1902, but there is conflicting evidence for her date of birth and, therefore, how old she was when she died. We have been unable to trace the registration of Ann's birth.

There are conflicting dates associated with the census record for 6 June 1841. *A Walk Around Elgar's Worcester* by K. E. L. and Marion Simmons (Elgar Society Journal, September 1985, p.19) states that Ann was 19 on this date, which would put her date of birth somewhere between 7 June 1821 and 6 June 1822. However, the website Genealogist.co.uk says she was 20, which would put her date of birth between 7 June 1820 and 6 June 1821.

The census for 3 April 1881 shows that 'Anne' (sic) was 58 on this date and born in 1823, which would imply a date of birth before 4 April 1823. The census for 5 April 1891 says that Ann was 68 and born in 1823, which agrees with the earlier census. However, the census for 31 March 1901 shows that Ann was 79 on this date and born in 1822, which suggests that her date of birth is sometime up to 31 March.

The Elgar family would presumably have seen to it that Ann's age at death on her mourning card, 80, was correct, which puts the birth in 1822 before September that year or in 1821 after 1 September. One burial record (the website Findagrave.com) says she was born in December 1822 and died at the age of 79. The *Worcester Journal* says that Ann was 81 when she died, which would put her birth in 1821 before September that year or in 1822 after 1 September. Significantly, Ann's baptismal entry at Hope Mansell Church is February 1822 (*Edward Elgar, His Life & Music* by Diana McVeagh). Ann's dates of birth therefore range from 7 June 1820 to 3 April 1823, giving her age at death 79, 80, 81 or 82!

We believe that Ann was born in January or February 1822 and she was thus 80 when she died on 1 September 1902.

Esther married Joseph Greening at Westbury-on-Severn on 26 May 1806. The church is dedicated to St Peter, St Paul and St Mary. A vast, almost cathedral-like building, it is surrounded by a large graveyard with a separate bell tower. Illust. 10 and Illust. 11 show Johannes Kip's engraving of Westbury-on-Severn and the church. It must have been a somewhat awesome experience for the couple at their wedding, walking down the very long central aisle towards the West Door.

It is interesting that the well-known writer Hannah More (see Chapter 12), who may have influenced Ann's mother, was brought up in the same region of England. It is said that Esther in old age closely resembled Hannah More (Illust. 12). In her scrapbook Ann posted a portrait of her and noted 'How like my own dear mother'. We presume she refers to a physical likeness. On the other hand, the features do not seem to resemble Ann's very much, so perhaps she meant that they were alike in something more – in character? If so, that would have been a considerable compliment, for Hannah More was a remarkable lady. She was a person of immense energy, intellect and wit, and, in addition, she was a social reformer, believing passionately in education for the poor. She set up 12 schools in the Mendip area, and today there are still a number of schools around Bristol named after her. In the 1790s she wrote several of her 'Cheap Repository Tracts' on moral, religious and political topics for distribution to the literate poor. It may not be too fanciful, therefore, to consider that ripples from Hannah More's important promotion of education for the poor and for girls should have reached the Severnside villages where Esther Apperley grew up. She could even perhaps have provided something of a role model for Esther.

The move to Weston-under-Penyard
After their marriage Joseph and Esther Greening went to live at a smallholding named *Handley* on the southern edge of the village of Pontshill near Weston-under-Penyard. This was only seven miles as the crow flies from Westbury, but it would have taken them at least two hours by pony and trap to cover the journey along the narrow winding lanes (Illust. 13).

Joseph may have been a tenant farmer to begin with, but it is possible that he came to own land. Perhaps the words on his headstone (Illust. 14) in Claines Churchyard, Worcester (on the north side of the church), suggest that he was more than a common labourer: 'late of *Handley* in the parish of Weston, Herefordshire'.

Handley was situated in beautiful countryside. Interestingly, just the year before Ann was born, William Cobbett, the journalist, traveller and political activist (1763-1835), stayed in one of the impressive Jacobean and Georgian houses near

1. Greenings & Apperleys

10. Johannes Kip's 1712 engraving of Westbury-on-Severn, showing the church where Ann's parents were married, the original late Elizabethan Westbury Court and Westbury Court Garden.

The Dutch water garden was laid out from 1696–1705 and, in modern times, restored and preserved by the National Trust. The Elizabethan manor house was demolished in the 1740s, a later Palladian mansion was built in its place, and this was replaced by a nineteenth-century house, which is no longer standing.

11. The Church of St Mary, St Peter & St Paul, Westbury-on-Severn, where Ann's parents married in 1806. The separate tower will be noted.

1. *Greenings & Apperleys*

12. *1822 portrait of Hannah More by Henry William Pickersgill (reproduced by permission of © The National Portrait Gallery, London). Hannah More was a religious writer, philanthropist, poet and playwright.*

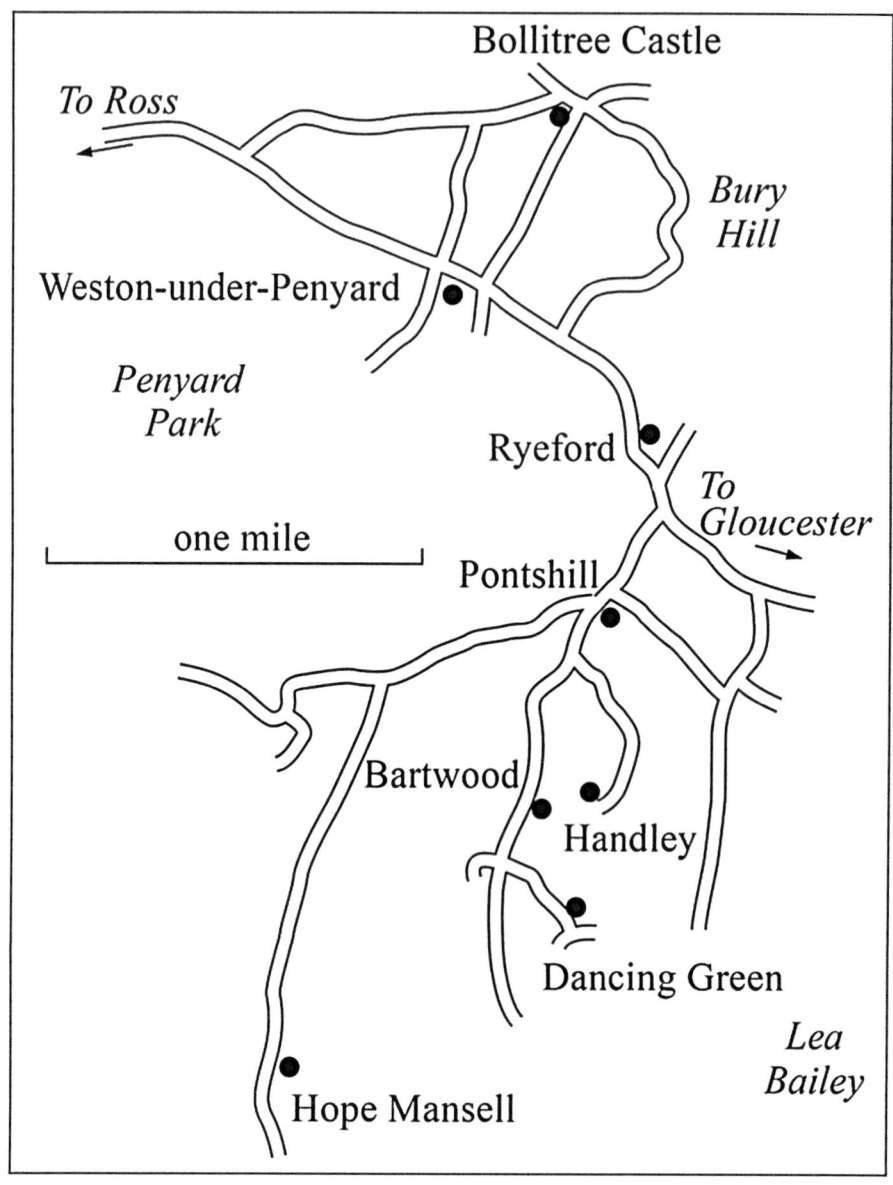

13. Map showing the districts around Weston-under-Penyard, Herefordshire.

1. Greenings & Apperleys

14. Grave of Ann's parents, Joseph & Esther Greening, Claines Churchyard, Worcester.

the village as the guest of William Palmer. *Bollitree Castle* near Weston-under-Penyard dates from around 1700 with older parts, and features castellated walls, turrets and a moat. Cobbett writes ecstatically about the area in his *Rural Rides*:

> *Nov 9-21, 1821, Gloucester to Burghclere*
>
> *I got to this beautiful place (Mr. William Palmer's) yesterday, from Gloucester. This is in the parish of Weston, two miles on the Gloucester side of Ross ... The spot where I now am is peculiarly well situated in all respects. The land very rich, the pastures the finest I ever saw, the trees of all kinds surpassing upon an average any that I have before seen in England. From the house, you see, in front and winding round to the left, a lofty hill, called Penyard Hill, at about a mile and a half distance, covered with oaks of the finest growth; along at the foot of this wood are fields and orchards continuing the slope of the hill down for a considerable distance, and, as the ground lies in a sort of ridges from the wood to the foot of the slope, the hill-and-dell is very beautiful ...*
>
> *Beneath Penyard Hill, and on one of the ridges before mentioned, is the parish church of Weston, with some pretty white cottages near it, peeping through the orchard and other trees; and coming to the paddock before the house are some of the largest and loftiest trees in the country, standing singly here and there, among which is the very largest and loftiest walnut-tree that I believe I ever saw, either in America or in England. In short, there wants nothing but the autumnal colours of the American trees to make this the most beautiful spot I ever beheld.*

2.
Ann's Childhood in Herefordshire, 1822-c.1840

Ann was the third child of the marriage of Joseph and Esther. Her older sister, Catherine Elizabeth, was born in 1808, 14 years before, and her brother John was born in 1815. There was quite a large gap between the three children, so perhaps Esther suffered miscarriages. A brother, William, was born five years after Ann; he died before he was two years old.

Ann was christened in the village of Hope Mansell, today a tiny, isolated hamlet, difficult to reach, as we know from researching for this book. Sitting in the churchyard one spring-like February afternoon amongst the snowdrops and listening to the chaffinch, wood pigeon and distant lowing of cattle, we felt very close to that world of nearly 200 years ago in which Ann grew up.

Opposite the thirteenth-century church is the fifteenth-century *Moat Farm*, which perhaps was once semi-fortified. It has now been lived in for generations by the same family. The farmer and his wife offered us a welcoming cup of tea, which made us feel very much at home.

The house on the edge of Pontshill in which Ann lived, *Handley* (Illust. 15), is now much changed (Illust. 16). Then it was a tiny cottage with a barn, surrounded by just over four acres of land. A large field of about two acres was bounded by pasture and a little orchard. Here Ann's lifelong and profound love of the countryside developed. Even today the area is very remote (Illust. 17).

The owner of the cottage, now enlarged and modernised, told us he had lived there for 44 years and his children had walked to the school in Weston-under-Penyard via a footpath across the fields which took them 20 minutes. This was almost certainly the same route that Ann would have taken 150 years earlier, had she gone to school here. Alternatively, there may have been a school at Pontshill, which would have been nearer to Ann's home. We cannot be sure.

The kind of education she received at school would have been limited. In a Victorian classroom children usually sat in rows, with the teacher at a desk, facing the class. It is likely that there would be maps and perhaps pictures on the walls. There would be a globe for geography lessons and an abacus to help with sums. Children wrote on slates with chalk, wiping them clean by spitting and rubbing with a coat sleeve or their finger! Slates could be used over and over. Children were taught the three Rs, very much by rote learning.

15. Handley, Ann's childhood home near Pontshill, Herefordshire, in 1928.

16. Handley in 2021, with May Hill in the distance and the wooded Lea Bailey enclosure to the right.

2. Ann's Childhood in Herefordshire, 1822-c.1840

17. Weston-under-Penyard from Handley. Ann would have looked out on smaller fields and more trees – and no pylons, of course.

Where Ann's consuming interest in books was born or conceived we really do not know. We can only assume that somewhere, some time in her childhood, books and encouragement to read them must have been given, probably by her mother. As stated, we have assumed from evidence that her father was illiterate, but Esther was certainly literate, and it would have been from her that the inspiration to read is most likely to have come. We have to make assumptions because how else did she come to devour books in the way she did? This is a question we cannot answer. It is a further possibility that she herself was inspired by the fairly local celebrity Hannah More who had very novel ideas about education.

It is strange that Ann, who was to become such an avid reader, should have had a father who appears to have been illiterate. Where provision of education is poor, some children manage to be reasonably educated in spite of the fact, perhaps as a result of innate curiosity, parental inspiration or a combination of the two. Luckily for her and her family – especially her son Edward – Ann fell into this category.

The impact that reading had on Ann was immense, illustrating what George Eliot wrote in a letter that men and women are 'imitative beings. We cannot, at least those who ever read to any purpose at all … help being modified by the ideas that pass through our minds.'

Ann's complete agreement with this is shown in the following extract in her scrapbook from a pamphlet by the novelist and historian Walter Besant on the value of novels:

Many of even the most eloquent upholders of novels miss the true reason of its popularity and usefulness. Novels take us out of ourselves ... What it must be to those whose struggle for existence is so sore. Whose humble place in the toiling vanguard of the great battle of life, to bid dull care be gone, and fly away to radiant lands where they may for an instant forget the pettiness and sordidness of the trivial round ... It is useless to be forever trying to induce the weary workman to improve his mind. He will do it so much more certainly and satisfactorily if he is not always treated as if he were a third-standard child. The company of the good and pure in the best fiction will ennoble him, will raise his ideals and broaden views narrowed by bitter experience, for after all, the great novelist is but a preacher in a rich and motley disguise.[1]

Ann's choice of extract is interesting in another aspect, implying that learning is to do with being inspired, rather than being compelled. People learn most effectively by being treated as capable of enquiry by themselves instead of doing what they are told. This is, of course, what Ann did. We may say that she was largely self-educated, just as Edward was to be.

We think the fact that Ann probably had little formal education paradoxically encouraged her to follow her own curiosity and interests. This she did for her whole life. Perhaps, indeed, education is not always a progressive force: it can often inhibit real thinking and feeling.

Ann may have had more education than we know about. Ann's daughter Lucy, in her unpublished memoirs entitled 'Reflections', states that Ann was well educated but she gives no indication of where or how. Even if so, we may conclude that the teaching she received was inspired. Otherwise, we can assume that it was native talent and interest in everything that carried her through.

Ann's home life must have offered her lively and enquiring mind much stimulus. Besides her love of books, she became skilled with her needle as we see from the sampler she produced in 1833 at the age of 10 or 11 (Illust. 18). She also became adept at drawing and writing poetry.

This is a riddle she wrote at the age of nine, an early example of her writing poetry:

My head is like a bulrush. It hangs very low,
And yet it is white as the driven snow.
My body is green as a greengage plum.
Tell me the riddle, I'll give you my thumb.

2. Ann's Childhood in Herefordshire, 1822-c.1840

18. Sampler of 1833 by Ann Greening.

3.
Ann's Youth & Early Adulthood, c.1840-1848

The family leave Herefordshire
Ann was probably about 18 years old when her parents moved to Worcester in around 1840, for we know from tithe records that Joseph was still at *Handley* in 1838. He was 60 in 1840 – elderly for those days. Ann may have preceded her parents in going to Worcester, for she would have finished her schooling several years earlier. It is not surprising that the Greenings left their smallholding, for this was the start of the Hungry Forties, a time of bad harvests and economic depression.

The older children, Elizabeth and John, had already left home for Worcester, a flourishing city where work could be found. It is possible that Esther's family had connections with Worcester and had helped them to make their way there. There is evidence of Apperleys living around the city, and we know that a cousin of Ann was employed at the *Shades Tavern* there in the 1840s.

In June 1834 Ann's sister, Elizabeth, married Francis Simmonds, and they lived at 22 Mealcheapen Street, close to The Cross, where markets were held. See Illust. 19 for a contemporary street plan of the district. (Mealcheapen, pronounced 'Melcheapen' by Worcester folk, means 'meal market'.) Francis Simmonds is described in a census as a builder, and in 1842 he had a carpentry and joinery business. Around 1843 he took over the running of the *Shades Tavern* at 16 Mealcheapen Street, apparently more of an eating place than an inn (Illust. 20).

John became a boot-maker in Worcester, one of almost 100 in the city then. He married Maria Kelley at Claines Parish Church (Illust. 21) on 4 April 1841, and within four years they had three children. John was only just able to support a growing family on his rather meagre wages, and this is probably why in 1847 he decided to emigrate to America. Percy Young writes that it was to her brother John's house, 'in idyllic surroundings near Claines', that Ann came.[1]

Research by K. E. L. and Marion Simmons[2] shows that the Greening parents were established 'between Northwick (Worcester) and Claines village' on census day, 1841, when the household consisted of Joseph, Esther and a girl, Martha (between 15 and 19) (i.e., not Ann). By 1845 the parents had gone to live at *Nucketts Farm*,[3] now called *Blossom Farm*, in Claines Parish, then a very large one situated in pleasant countryside and healthier than the centre of Worcester, which had been subject to serious cholera epidemics. Like *Handley* their new home

3. Ann's Youth & Early Adulthood, c.1840-1848

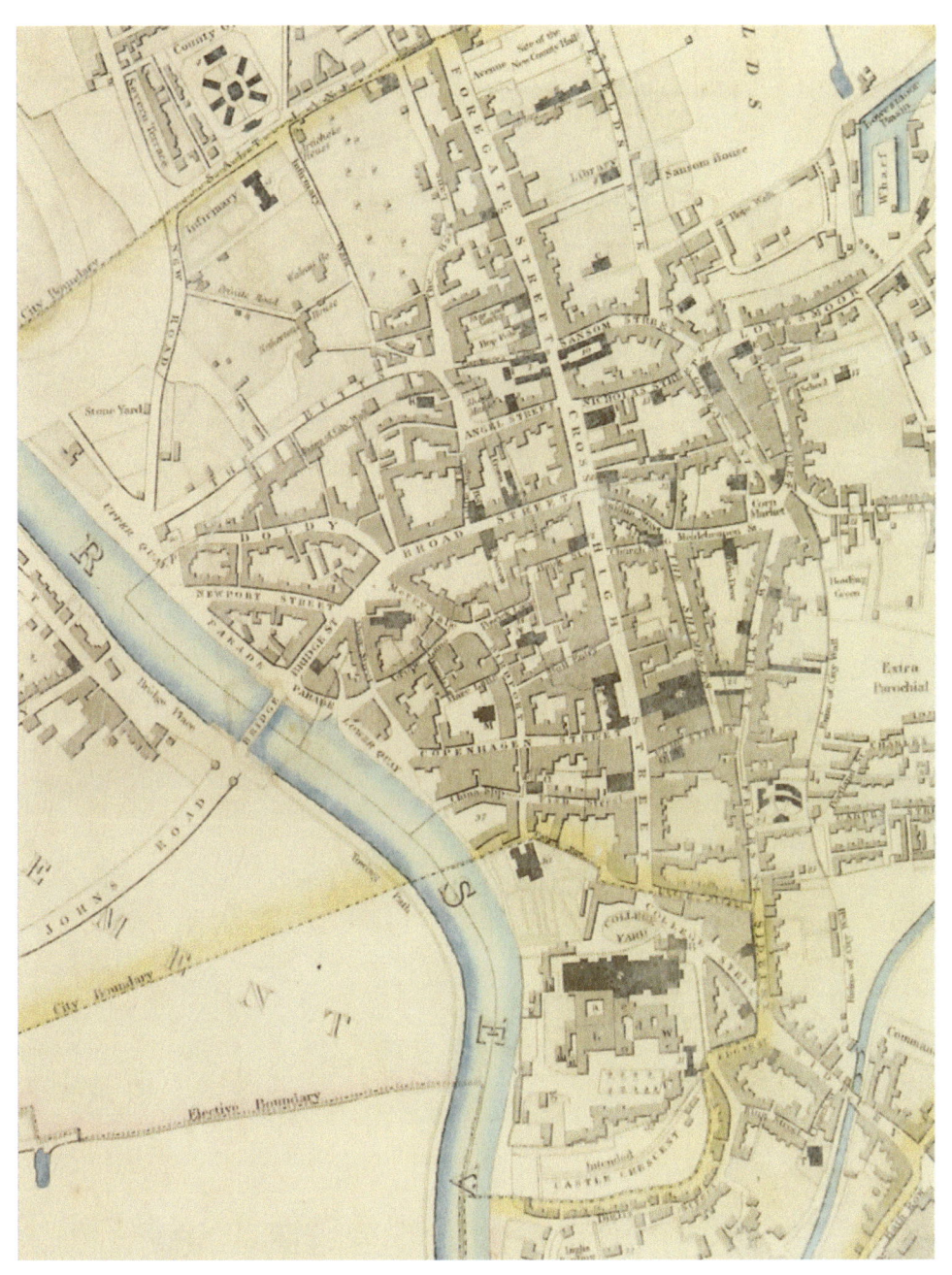

19. Part of Charles Crisp's 1832 'Plan of the City of Worcester' (reproduced by permission of Worcestershire Archive & Archaeology Service, Worcestershire County Council).

20. The former Shades Tavern, 16 Mealcheapen Street, Worcester; the original ground floor must be imagined.

Old Worcester, People & Places *by H. W. (Bill) Gwilliam sets the scene:* 'This imposing house, almost opposite the Reindeer Inn, was the Shades Inn, but originally, it was the home of the Russell family, one of the principal families of the City … It became a coffee house, then the Shades Tavern, the first city post office, then a bank, and in the 20th century, back again to an inn, using the old name of The Shades.'

3. Ann's Youth & Early Adulthood, c.1840-1848

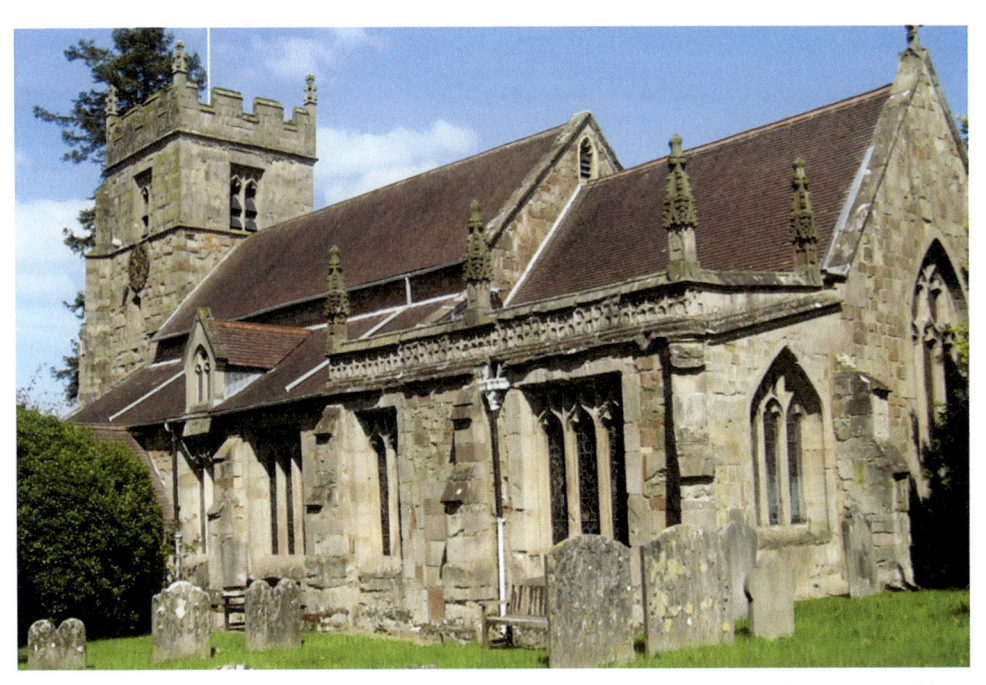

21. St John the Baptist's Church, Claines, Worcester, where Ann's parents are buried.

22. Nucketts Farm *(now* Blossom Farm), *Chatley, the Greenings' first home in Worcestershire.*

(Illust. 22) was fairly remote. We do not know if Ann ever lived with her parents at *Nucketts Farm*. In view of its distance from Worcester, it would have been very inconvenient for her work in the city.

Ann's arrival in Worcester
We may safely say that Ann's schooling in Weston-under-Penyard, such as it was, had finished by the time she went to Worcester, so finding employment (and perhaps, looking ahead, a husband) was the main consideration for her. She grew up in a world in which women were treated very differently from men, and it was assumed that their role centred round the home, with a life of domesticity before them. There was schooling for girls as well as boys, but it was regarded as less important, and far fewer opportunities were available. All the home-making skills would have been taught to girls, including cooking, laundering, housekeeping, keeping the home clean, sewing, dress-making and mending. Non-essential activities pursued for enjoyment included drawing, writing, poetry and musical skills, ranging from the very simple to the ability to play instruments.

The notion of separate spheres of influence affected all levels of class. In some ways, working-class or lower middle-class girls brought up in the country had a good deal more freedom than girls who were children of the gentry and were therefore required to conform to more regularised expectations. From this Ann would have benefited, because for the first 12 years of her life she lived in a remote country setting, surrounded by the beauty of the natural world, which she was free to explore in a way that was often difficult or impossible for urban children. She could learn to be independent to some degree, make decisions for herself and dream of what a worthwhile life should consist of.

On arrival in Worcester all this changed for Ann. She seems to have had to earn her keep by working as a maid at her brother-in-law's inn in Mealcheapen Street in the centre of Worcester. It is likely, however, that she lived out at Claines for some of the time, which would have offered a more kindly transition from rural to urban life for her. Unfortunately, we know very little about her life as a young woman; we have no indication of any further schooling she might have received. Almost certainly she did not have any particular career in mind, such as the ones that were then open to women: teaching, being a governess, nurse or seamstress, or indeed straightforward manual work such as employment in a glover's factory. (Worcester was synonymous with glove-making in the nineteenth century.)

Whether Ann was happy in this move to a city, country-lover as she was, we shall never know. It was a move, however, that was to change her life beyond anything she might have imagined. Instead of exploring the fields and woods in solitude she found herself in new situations among strangers.

3. *Ann's Youth & Early Adulthood, c.1840-1848*

23. William Elgar's 1845 map, showing directions from Worcester to Nucketts Farm, Chatley.
   'Mrs Greening' is at the top, 'Claines Church' at the centre and Worcester at the bottom.

We do know that, when Elizabeth was running the *Shades Tavern*, Ann went to help her sister. This was presumably where she met William Elgar, a piano-tuner from Dover. It seems clear that William arrived in Worcester as early as 1841[4] and lodged with the Greenings for a period, since his 1845 map showing how to get to *Nucketts Farm* (Illust. 23) is annotated 'From Worcester Cross to Mrs Greenings', implying that he regarded Esther Greening as his landlady. The 12-mile round trip to Worcester (a walk of at least four hours) made *Nucketts Farm* at Chatley an impractical place to live for both Ann and William, and either or both may have moved later to the *Shades Tavern*. Through the mid-1840s Ann and William became attracted to each other, but we know nothing of their courtship. We can be assured of one quality of Ann that doubtless attracted William: Elgar biographer Basil Maine writes:

Upon all who met her, she left the impression of being a remarkable woman. She walked with such grace of movement as to seem out of touch with the earth.[5]

Ann was in no hurry: the several years of friendship between her and William before marriage may be seen in the light of the following observation by Ann in a remarkable journal ('Worcester Papers') that we discuss later:

How much anxiety and misery might be avoided in the world if people were always to take the precaution to choose their partner as they would choose their weather-garb – by selecting such an article as would produce comfort in a storm, and one that would remain untarnished by a good soaking.

William Henry Elgar
William Henry Elgar (Illust. 24) (1821-1906) was, according to Basil Maine, a man of small build and delicate features, whose reputation as a piano-tuner was considerable and who would ride a horse to his tuning engagements.[6] There would be plenty of opportunities for such a lifestyle, for before long he was offered the post of piano-tuner at *Witley Court*, the seat of Lord Dudley and where the Dowager Queen Adelaide, widow of King William IV, resided from 1843 to 1846.

William was clearly very able musically and was a more than proficient violinist, pianist and organist. Lord Dudley, on hearing him play the piano one day after he had tuned it, offered to pay for his tuition to become a professional pianist, but he was too nervous to accept the offer.[7] However, he certainly enjoyed playing in the various amateur groups around Worcester and fulfilling playing and teaching

24. *William Elgar, aged about 35 (1856).*

engagements in the county. In 1842[8] an important post became his, that of organist at the Roman Catholic Church of St George in Worcester. Here his duties included training the choir as well as playing for all the services. (Some 40 years later St George's would replace William and, after a year or two, appoint his son Edward.)

Maine writes:

> *As a musician, W. H. Elgar was accomplished, for not only did he play the organ at St George's, but, whenever the Meeting of the Three Choirs took place in Worcester, he played among the violins. He was also an expert pianoforte-tuner and in that capacity often visited Witley Court when Queen Adelaide was staying there. The tuning of pianofortes may not appear to be anything more than an ordinary accomplishment at this present time when tuners are required to put in order seven or eight pianos a day. But at that time, a tuner would devote half-a-day to a single instrument. W. H. Elgar's reputation as a tuner was considerable, partly because he practised the craft with art and patience, partly because it was his habit to ride upon a thoroughbred horse to the houses that had out-of-tune pianos. His influence in the musical life of the city and county can be judged by the fact the Three Choirs added several works to their repertory on his recommendation. One of his descendants has described him as a man of small build and with features so delicate that he should have been a girl. His temperament seems to have been what used to be contemptuously described as artistic. His business was never a great success for the simple reason that he was disinclined to attend to the necessary book-keeping. By no stretch of the imagination could he be described as a business man.*[9]

William could turn his hand to composition too. Elgar biographer Percy Young notes that 'he had the habit, which Edward also had, of carrying sketch books about him on his country excursions' and that once, when father and son were forced to shelter from the rain under a tree, William noted down 'some passing inspiration'. He conceded that his mind wandered.[10] Young considered that William, along with his Kentish family, 'possessed an impish quality, a capacity to comment on people and affairs allusively', which he passed on to some of his children.[11]

Lucy in her 'Reflections' notes that her father was 'blessed with a well-regulated mind, and undisturbed by that unbalancing element known as genius. He was a musician of great ability, and a distinguished man without having become so by the production of any work of distinction ...'

William had enthusiastic correspondence with his family back in Dover, and this led to his brother Thomas Elgar (1826-1911) coming to Worcester. In 1845 Tom Elgar painted a humorous picture of life at the *Shades Tavern*: Ann is shown

3. Ann's Youth & Early Adulthood, c.1840-1848

25. *Ann at the Shades Tavern, Worcester, by Tom Elgar. It will be noted that Tom has misspelt Ann.*

working there (Illust. 25). Tom's sister Susanna (1817-1887) also visited Worcester around this time; it seems she formed an illicit attachment with the landlord Francis Simmonds, who was, of course, Ann's brother-in-law. We can only imagine what Ann and Elizabeth thought about that. By 1847 Susanna Elgar was back in Kent, where she gave birth to an illegitimate son, James Henry Elgar. However, Susanna returned to Worcester at some stage and died there in 1887, having married 20 years previously.[12]

One other member of the Elgar family came to live in Worcester. William's brother Henry Elgar (1832-1917) became his apprentice and lived in Worcester on and off during the 1850s but was a permanent resident after 1860. Percy Young records that he was a competent musician, was for many years organist of two churches in Malvern, and remained in the Elgar music business until his death in 1917.[13] Henry was also an inveterate theatre-goer, an enthusiasm that he passed on to his nephew Edward.

4.
Marriage & Family Life, 1848-1863

Early years in Worcester, 1848-1856
On 19 January 1848 Ann married William Henry Elgar. They were both aged 26. Surprisingly this took place in St Mary's Church in Islington rather than in the parish church at Claines, where the family had settled. Why Islington is an unsolved mystery. Did Ann's father disapprove of his daughter marrying a mere piano-tuner? Perhaps William still had friends in London, where he had trained, and possibly godparents.

Two months after Ann was married, her brother, John, wrote to her from America on 14 March 1848:

My own dear Sister Ann,

I suppose long ere this you are a wife. May heaven shower its choicest blessings on you. May an over-ruling Providence guide you through the mazes of a chequered life. May you enjoy a long life and more happiness than usually falls to the lot of mortals. It is the sincerest wish and prayer that was ever breathed by your only brother. You must imagine my feelings towards you; to describe them is impossible. Tell the man you have chosen to spend life's weary journey with, and whom I now call Brother, to love you for me ... I shall certainly see you all again if ever I can find some cargo to pay my journey. At present I must be content and wait patiently. God knows how long. Keep my dear parents alive until then. I've got 6000 miles to separate you and faults (?) are lost. Their names are sacred and thoughts of them are Holy. God bless them and all of you.

The cold is still intense. It freezes water to ice in a minute. Still I work out in it and it is endurable. We are so far inland and so great an elevation above the sea that we breathe a different air to you. It's almost all oxygen and hydrogen, very little nitrogen, consequence everything dries up instantly. Salt never gets damp. Iron don't rust and wood decays with dry-rot. We use much salt, and the animals must have some often for, being so far from the sea, we have no saline particles in the air like your little island, which is saturated with salt.

Perhaps Ann drew from this letter the consolation that, no matter what hardships married life had in store for her, she was not far from her parents and sister and was unlikely to have to endure such physical hardships as her brother.

4. Marriage & Family Life, 1848-1863

Illust. 26 shows Ann in 1848, around the time of her marriage.

Ann and William initially lived in Claines but moved to 2 College Precincts (then known as 2 College Yard), very close to Worcester Cathedral. The Georgian house was three-storeyed with no garden or land attached to it, standing in a row of similar houses. The surrounding area was narrow and cramped, close to the Lychgate (demolished for redevelopment in the 1960s).

The first years of their marriage in Worcester must have been an exceptionally busy time for Ann. Her first child, Henry John ('Harry'), was born on 15 October 1848. Only nine days later, Ann's father, Joseph, died in Lowesmoor, Worcester, on 24 October, aged 68. Ann's widowed mother, Esther, then went to live with them, where she died on 2 March 1852, aged 63 (she was buried with her husband in Claines Churchyard). So Ann's past life had been taken from her in a very short space of time. She does seem to have been very fond of her parents, and we know from a letter which her brother, John, sent from Wisconsin how much he too felt the loss. It is not too much to imagine that her own warm relationship with her children derived from that with her own parents.

1852 was the year when Ann became a Roman Catholic. She had received instruction from the priest at St George's Roman Catholic Church, where William played the organ on Sundays. It is said that she started going to church in order to accompany William on the long walk from Claines to St George's. She could have gone to a nearby Protestant Church, but worshippers at St George's may well have been friendly towards her as the wife of their organist, and their welcome may have roused her interest in Roman Catholicism.

Later in 1852 Ann had an addition to the family with the birth of her first daughter, Lucy Ann, on 29 May. Her delight was expressed in the poem she wrote at that time for her husband, evidence of a creative outlook on life which was to be inherited by Edward.

Another child is born, another guest,
Elgar, to thy domestic hearth is given;
Receive her as a precious boon from heaven,
And while thine eyes with a father's fondness rest
On thy fair babe, reposing on the breast
Of her, thy lov'd wife, whose smile
Can all the cares of busy life beguile.
Be in her love and in thy children blest –
Yet, ah, be mindful that 'tis Heaven's behest
With added blessings duty's claims increase:
Train up thy children in the paths of peace,

26. Photograph of Ann, aged about 26 at the time of her marriage (1848).

4. Marriage & Family Life, 1848-1863

Be Christian precepts on their minds impress'd,
Then shall their upright walk, o'er life's rough stage
Solace thine anxious heart in thy declining age.
August 25, 1852[1]

It would be interesting to know what William's reaction to her poem was. We know that he had no time for religion at this time and can imagine his strong discouragement of any such conversion. He only played the organ in the church to earn money and is reputed to have vacated the organ seat often during the long sermons to quench his thirst at the Hop Market!

We wonder sometimes whether theirs was an ideal marriage or rather one that had to be worked at, although it certainly sprang from love: Lucy tells of how excited they all were at Broadheath when Father came home at the end of his working week (1856-1859).

There are many indications in their later life, however, that Ann needed to draw on a good deal of tolerance and understanding. Edward's close friend Hubert Leicester remembered that 'the old man was a regular terror as regards the Catholicity of his family – used to threaten to shoot his daughters if caught going to confession.'[2]

Elgar biographer Jerrold Northrop Moore comments, however, that 'it was all noise and bluff: his wife went quietly on her way, using her tact and kindness to reconcile her husband to raising all the children as Roman Catholics.'[3] They and she were baptised at the Catholic Church.

That William's raging against the Catholicism in his family was noise and bluff is backed up by the following philosophical thoughts of his which show him to be in awe of women. Although he is apparently writing here of women in general, we feel these lines were conditioned by one woman in particular, his wife.

Women are not unlike the flowers of the forest on a tempestuous day – whilst all else in the wide domain is contentious, and discordant, and warring, they still remain the same practical, beauteous and submissive objects of our admiration.

A woman's frown is capable of bringing a man to a proper sense of duty sooner than the points of a thousand bayonets.

Were there no women there would be no love; were there no love, there would be no happiness; were there no happiness, there would be nought but dreariness, and dismay and misery. So that it may be said that from the female sex springs all that is good, and virtuous and honourable. In short, a woman is a particle of the Great Fountain of all goodness, from which is constantly gushing forth a torrent of pure, holy love.

These lines of William's appeared in the remarkable handwritten journals he wrote with Ann entitled, 'Worcester Papers'.

One more child was born during the Elgars' first stay at 2 College Precincts: Pollie (Susanna Mary) arrived on 28 December 1854.

Broadheath, 1856-1859

The Elgars found Worcester a lively city. Even so, Ann longed so much to return to a country life that she persuaded William to rent a cottage known as *The Firs* in the hamlet of Broadheath, about three miles from Worcester to the west and reached by winding muddy lanes. They moved there from College Precincts in 1856. This was perhaps because another child was on the way. It is likely though that Ann was concerned about the health of her family, whilst living in a city that was notoriously insanitary. The quiet and natural surroundings of Broadheath must have been congenial to her, yet she must have felt somewhat isolated, especially when her husband was away in town on business. Elgar biographer Basil Maine wrote:

> *Her world was small and lonely. It consisted of the tiny house and garden. Her mind, however, needed a larger world and it was through the reading of books that it found escape.*[4]

This part of Ann's story is well documented. Edward was born at Broadheath on 2 June 1857. His five-year-old sister Lucy vividly recalls the day in her collection of memories called 'Reflections':

> *How well I remember the day he was born! The air was sweet with the perfume of flowers, bees were humming, and all the earth was lovely. There seemed to be, to we little ones, a lot of unnecessary running about in the house, and Father came tearing up the drive with a strange man in the carriage. And before that, an old lady whom we had never seen there before arrived with a large bag, and we were told by the younger maid there was a baby in that bag! That was good enough for our weak comprehension, and so we were taken a scamper across the heath to be out of the way.*

We have a valuable crayon drawing of the cottage in 1856 by John Chessell Buckler (1793-1894) (Illust. 27). It is likely to be an accurate portrayal because Buckler was a distinguished architect. We can only speculate how he came to be interested in drawing such a simple building. Perhaps William had met him in Worcester Cathedral, where Buckler had restored some of the fabric, or perhaps

4. Marriage & Family Life, 1848-1863

it was at *Witley Court*. The picture is fascinating, as it shows all the members of the family, including William's younger brother Henry, who had become his apprentice and had built the stable block to house William's pony, Jack. William himself created a special pathway where the children could bowl their hoops.

Lucy writes about her time at Broadheath:

My Mother was not in a way called musical, though her calm, high-thinking mind could fully appreciate the nice little musical evenings we so often had in those early days, and her sweet voice blended beautifully with the others. For

27. Crayon drawing of 1856 by John C. Buckler of the Elgars' cottage at Broadheath (The Firs), Worcester, just before Edward was born there.

Father very frequently brought their friends from Worcester for an evening or a week-end. And well I remember a dear man we all loved, and who was a constant visitor, named Allen, a solicitor – and another named Leicester, John Leicester, a tall man who sang in the choir at Church.

Well, they were thoroughly happy in our cottage home, and sang and sang for the very joy of singing. And Mr Allen always (yes, every time he came) would sing to Father's accompaniment, 'Di Provenza il mar'[5] – oh! I can hear it now! We got to know every note of it by heart. Also we knew every note of the glee 'Mynheer Van Duncke' with which they finished up and all sang together. It was lovely. And we three little ones sat on a sofa to listen, and of course thoroughly enjoyed ourselves – but dared scarcely move or blink our eyes, for fear of attracting attention and being sent to bed! So we were brought up in the very atmosphere of happiness and simple enjoyment of life. As I became older and understood more of life, I seemed always to be studying – Mother's grace and manners, her whole appearance indeed indicated a mood of serene pleasure – that delightful air of cheerful happiness which surrounds those who can enjoy ordinary life without the excitement of passion or appetite.

I well recall how beautifully she read and recited poetry, and would so often gather us round her with baby Edward on her knee and tell us sweet stories, one of which we liked better than some was **Speak gently** *and the poems of Mrs Hemans[6],* **The Better Land***, we never tired listening to – and so our sunny life went on and we were ever studying in our grateful ways the truth of Mother's character, the naturalness of her mind, and the simplicity and variety of her tasks which made her so happy in all the situations of her life. Her quiet thoughtful disposition seemed to be imbued into our own being – and I used to gaze on her noble, amiable face and think 'Are there any cares, I wonder?'*

And yet with all her sweetness and charm she could, to we children, be very severe if we were in the wrong and put on a forbidding tone and a look in her eye of microscopic power which was positively paralising (sic) and gave us horrid little shivers. But the scoldings never lasted long, and what we learnt we never forgot. She taught us that as we all have our wearisome hours which cannot always be cast aside by an effort of the will, it is not wise to encourage the feeling of discontent – or as others may put it, temper.

She always held the absolute belief that all which happens to a good person happens for the best, and whatever is given has proved to be the very thing which is needed, the thing worth having, if we put our small helpless hands into the Hands of Compassion, the guiding guarding Hands, we shall be lifted up and strengthened for all we have to do. We then understood by her reassuring and gentle talks, any life which progresses must learn the meaning of a crisis, of turning points, of disappointments, and so left our daily life in wider horizons and other's experiences.

Lucy wrote that Edward in his earliest years 'was entranced by the sound of his mother's voice as it rose and fell, the *sound* of the words as they flowed in well-turned phrases, and the *sound* of the rhymes and the metrical rhythm he quickly learned to appreciate in the poetry to which he listened.'

Perhaps the most interesting photograph of Ann comes from this period. We felt compelled to use it on the front cover. It was taken in 1859 and shows the young Edward on her lap (Illust. 28).

Return to Worcester, 1859-1863

Lucy in her 'Reflections' writes about their time at Broadheath as idyllic, so why should the family return to Worcester when Edward was still only two years old? Two reasons might have been that another child was on the way (Frederick Joseph) and the Broadheath cottage was too small to accommodate any more. Later, at 10 High Street, there was a servant/nurse, Matilda Knott ('Kit'), who was with the Elgars for many years. (A handyman ex-actor, Ned Spiers, worked at the shop, but we think he lived elsewhere with his wife.[7]) A third possible reason for the move is, however, likely – the inconvenience of living out in the country for William's growing business.

In addition to tuning pianos William had become interested in selling pianos. This was encouraged by a good friend of his, whom he had met at the Glee Club. John Leicester (Lucy's 'tall man who sang in the choir at Church') belonged to a well-established and affluent Catholic Worcester family, and it was through Leicester that William had become organist at St George's Roman Catholic Church, giving him a secure though modest income. Now it was John Leicester who nudged William into setting up a business, and Leicester's brother, also William, offered his printing shop at 6 High Street as a place where William Elgar could sell pianos.

The family therefore moved back to Worcester in 1859. Their first house, where Joe was born, was 1 Edgar Street near the cathedral. (This was demolished later in the nineteenth century for the widening of Severn Street.) It had no garden for the children to play in. (It has been suggested that they romped around in the nearby grounds of the cathedral, but Edward, speaking to the Friends of Worcester Cathedral in 1932, said they were not allowed to make the passage through the cathedral into the cloisters or among the graves.)

28. Photograph of Ann with Edward, 1859.

4. Marriage & Family Life, 1848-1863

At William Leicester's printing shop at 6 High Street William Elgar may have sold sheet music and small instruments. Moreover, William had taken up John Leicester's suggestion to sell pianos. On experiencing some success, he had become convinced of its potential, so in December 1859 he asked his brother Henry to join him to create the Elgar Brothers company, though not as an equal but rather as an employee. Henry was then 27 years old and very different in temperament from William, but, nevertheless, he agreed. It was not an easy arrangement: Henry was much more practically minded than William, and for some years there were disputes between the brothers as Henry struggled to make William more business-like in his approach.

The new business partnership must have had considerable impact on Ann. William Leicester's son Hubert later recalled that she 'worried as to where the money was coming from.'[8]

In 1861 Ann had yet another move to negotiate – back to 2 College Precincts. A younger brother for Edward, Frank (Francis Thomas), was born here. This was Hilary's grandfather, and he was greeted with great joy as a very healthy baby.

Two years later sadly, Ann's sister, Elizabeth, died. Her marriage had been a chequered one as already mentioned. Following the departure of Susanna Elgar, life resumed a more straightforward course. After her husband's death in 1862 Elizabeth continued to run the *Shades* on her own. She died a few months later, and there were no children of the marriage to mourn her.

We do not know how close the sisters were, and there was a considerable age difference between them. Nonetheless, her death would have been a great sadness, for it was due to Elizabeth that Ann came to live in Worcestershire. Yet another link with her early years was gone.

5.
Life at 10 High Street, 1863-1878
(first 15 years)

In 1863 the Elgar family moved yet again – to 10 High Street, Worcester (Illust. 29). These were much larger premises, with two storeys for a shop and living accommodation on two storeys above. It was well located, on the narrow part of High Street (now wider) and not far from the cathedral. Here Elgar Brothers Pianoforte & Music Warehouse was set up.

As Hubert Leicester, Edward's friend who lived four doors away, remembered: 'At the back there was a long courtyard containing the workshop where the piano repairs and polishing were done, and at the end of this long courtyard a cottage which was often let to … men employed by W.H.E. for special polishing. They were very often foreigners, who were as a matter of course musical and played some instrument.'[1]

It was a very propitious time for such an enterprise. Most cities had a number of music shops selling pianos, and the Elgar music business was in fact one of several flourishing in Worcester at this time. See Box B, The Piano in Victorian Society.

Illust. 30 shows the Georgian houses around 10 High Street (on the left) in 1860. Worcester Cathedral dominates the area. The house and surroundings would have been very busy. See Box C, Worcester, A Lively City. How happy Ann was at moving here is a matter of conjecture, for it may have been considered a loss in social status to be living above a shop like any tradesman. She would have had steep stairs to negotiate as well, and she was well advanced in another pregnancy, for Dot (Helen Agnes) was born in 1864 soon after the move. Of her six children in 1863 three were under six years old. Harry, the eldest, was 14, and the girls, Lucy and Pollie, were 11 and eight. (An abbreviated family tree is shown in Illust. 31.)

Although the lower two floors on the premises had large and airy rooms, these were used for the business, and Ann and her family had to manage with smaller rooms at the top of the house. Opening the windows to let in more air would only add to the noisy and noisome nature of life within the four walls.

Because the house was on a narrow stretch of the High Street, sounds would be magnified. Then there would be the foul air of drains and horses and many

5. Life at 10 High Street, 1863-1878 (first 15 years)

29. The Elgar Brothers music shop at 10 High Street, Worcester, c.1910. Note the tram rails and overhead wires.

Ann Greening: Mother of Edward Elgar

30. The cathedral end of High Street, Worcester, c.1860 (Rock & Company engraving). 10 High Street is on the left-hand side.

48

5. Life at 10 High Street, 1863-1878 (first 15 years)

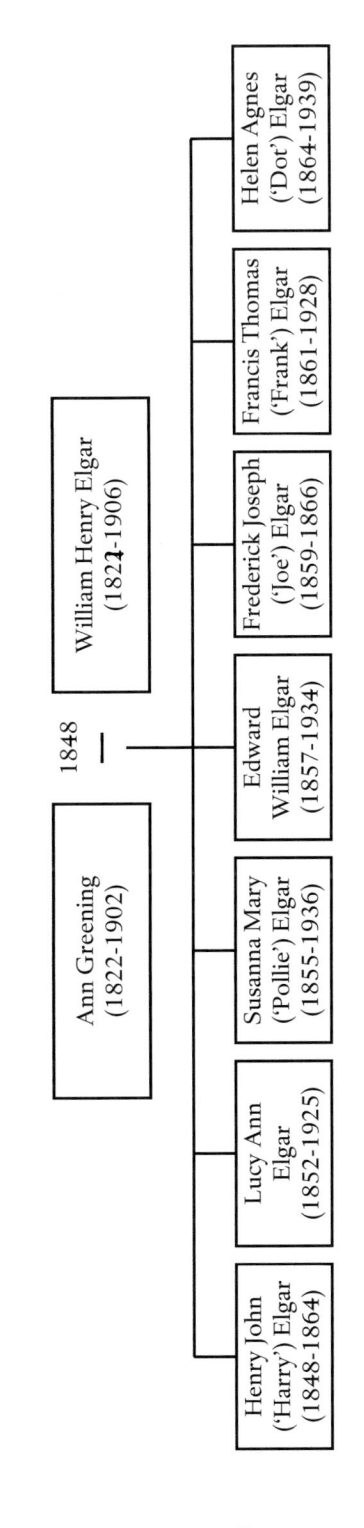

31. Abbreviated Elgar family tree (two generations).

Ann Greening (1822-1902) — 1848 — William Henry Elgar (1821-1906)

- Henry John ('Harry') Elgar (1848-1864)
- Lucy Ann Elgar (1852-1925)
- Susanna Mary ('Pollie') Elgar (1855-1936)
- Edward William Elgar (1857-1934)
- Frederick Joseph ('Joe') Elgar (1859-1866)
- Francis Thomas ('Frank') Elgar (1861-1928)
- Helen Agnes ('Dot') Elgar (1864-1939)

other sources of pollution. What a sea-change this was for Ann after the space and freedom she had enjoyed at Broadheath. Her thoughts must often have returned to the memories of life in the days at the cottage, where she was surrounded by birds and trees, rather than by the noise and bustle of a busy high street.

Gone were the days when she could walk out through the cottage door into her own garden. Now she was separated from the outside world by steep stairs. Shopping, talking to neighbours, just enjoying some fresh air on a lovely day was something to be planned in advance. It is possible, therefore, that she experienced a certain amount of claustrophobia and longing for the past. Being Ann Greening, however, she would not have allowed herself to wallow in self-pity.

William and Ann's children were growing up, and there was schooling to see to. Around 1860 Lucy and Pollie were sent to a Catholic 'Dame School' at 11 Britannia Square, Worcester, run by Miss Caroline Walsh; Edward joined them in 1863.

5. Life at 10 High Street, 1863-1878 (first 15 years)

Box B: The Piano in Victorian Society

The mid-Victorian era saw great changes in the economic outlook for middle-class people. Interestingly the sale of pianos was taken by one scholar recently as the clearest example of the changes, 'From the 1820s the piano had become the key status item in the typical middle-class home and had replaced the dining table as the most expensive object.' (Susie Steinbach, *Understanding the Victorians: Politics, Culture & Society in Nineteenth-Century Britain*, 2017, 2nd edition, p.109.)

Whilst earlier owning a piano had been a symbol only of a very wealthy and cultured class, by the 1860s the development in manufacturing techniques meant that, instead of being an expensive craftsman-created commodity, pianos could be mass-produced in Britain, with more relatively cheap German and American pianos becoming available.

The piano became popular not only as a status symbol but also as a major source of entertainment centred on the home. Many people became quite musically proficient and good players enjoyed making music. Sheet music was now plentiful and inexpensive, and music stools and metronomes much more affordable. Parallel to developments in the production of reading matter – novels, newspapers and magazines – music benefited from the arrival of machine-made paper, the rotary steam press and power-binding.

As the 1860s and 1870s progressed, piano ownership spread even further down the social scale to the lower middle class, though it remained firmly out of the reach of the working class until later in the century. By the time Queen Victoria died, however, owning a piano was becoming popular generally.

Box C: Worcester, A Lively City

Worcester was a lively city in which to live. With a population of 30,000 in 1831 (it reached 46,000 by the end of the century), it was fairly prosperous because of its china and glove manufacturing and some engineering. Its cathedral and especially the Three Choirs Festival, held there every three years, brought many visitors. Intellectually and culturally, it had much to offer. *Berrow's Worcester Journal* claims to be the oldest newspaper in the world still in publication, starting from a news-sheet in 1690.

In 1842 there were three 'music and musical instruments sellers' listed in a trade directory. In 1869 there were three listed piano-tuners and two piano warehouses, Elgar Brothers at 10 High Street and Charles Baldwyn at 101 High Street. In 1885 there were five piano-tuners, including W. H. Elgar, and six piano warehouses, including another in High Street.

It is interesting how families of enterprising traders, such as the Elgars, contributed to artistic life in various ways. The Baldwyns were another example. The competing piano warehouse-proprietor Charles Baldwyn preceded William Elgar as organist of St George's Roman Catholic Church. His brother Henry, piano-tuner and harpist, had a son, Charles Henry Clifford Baldwyn, who played the violin but found fame as a popular Royal Worcester Porcelain artist, famous for his renditions of small birds and landscapes. Henry Baldwyn had a younger son, Edgar, pianist and violinist, and a daughter, Maud, pianist, composer, songwriter – and lifelong friend of Edward Elgar. Charles Henry Clifford Baldwyn's grandson Rodney Baldwyn was organist of Pershore Abbey for 30 years (and one-time secretary of the Elgar Society).

There had been a significant interest in the book trade in Worcester since the mid-eighteenth century, when the Lewis family ran a book business. After 1836 Mrs Anne Deighton set up a public library at 53 High Street; Ann Elgar would have had easy access to this. In 1842 there were 22 'booksellers, binders and stationers' in Worcester and 10 libraries, which we presume to have been run on a subscription basis. If Ann had had the money, she could have had access to a large number of books and periodicals. In 1869 there were 28 stationers, 23 booksellers, eight publishers, five circulating libraries and two reading rooms. (Edward Spark ran the Worcester Railway Library Institute and John Evans the Working Men's Hall, Refreshment and Reading Room.) In 1885 there were five publishers, three circulating libraries, 18 newsagents and 21 booksellers. Ann's love of reading could therefore have been well met.

5. Life at 10 High Street, 1863-1878 (first 15 years)

Box C continued

When William Elgar arrived in Worcester from Dover in 1841, he came by horse-drawn stagecoach. Within a decade he would have been able to come much more quickly and comfortably by rail. Worcester's first railway station at Shrub Hill was opened in 1850 and belonged to the Oxford, Worcester & Wolverhampton Railway and the Midland Railway. Worcester Foregate Street station was opened by the Great Western Railway in 1860. The railway had a transformative effect on British society as well as on commerce and industry. The young Edward Elgar travelled by train to London for the day to hear the latest musical works performed.

After listing a number of amenities, such as a natural history society, a literary and scientific Athenaeum in Foregate Street and numerous musical societies, such as the Madrigal Society, the Glee Club and the Instrumental Society, Percy Young writes:

> *The Elgars lived in the middle of all these activities ... and were doubtless content to believe that theirs was a remarkable cultural environment. William must also have appreciated the tangible rewards that came to him in the shape of fees for piano-tuning and fiddling. (Elgar, O.M., 1955, p.27.)*

Charles Crisp's 1832 map of Worcester (Illust. 20) shows a part-medieval, part-Georgian city, after the coming of the canal in 1815 but before the railway, a time of gradually accelerating industrialisation and growth. Stagecoaches from London came into Sidbury and up the newly built College Street (still only single-carriageway) that had intruded into the peace of the cathedral's College Yard by 1816 (according to a map by T. Eaton). To cross the Severn at Worcester Bridge and travel onwards to Wales, stagecoaches had to negotiate a maze of medieval streets, through which Deansway was pushed in 1941, causing the disappearance of Merry Vale, Grope Lane, Birdport, Hare Lane and China Slip. In 1832 the river largely bounded Worcester to the west, the city wall to the east (the surviving part of this now runs parallel to a twentieth-century relief road). Some of the old street and district names captivated Edward Elgar in his youth: Birdport, Dolday (shown incorrectly by Crisp as Doldy) and Diglis. This is the Worcester to which his mother and father came and met.

Box C continued

By studying Crisp's map and the several books of old photographs of Worcester that are available, one may conjure up in the imagination something of the old city. Specifically, we may find on the map where Ann lived:

- 2 College Precincts (was 2 College Yard), 1848 to 1856
- (Broadheath, 1856 to 1859)
- 1 Edgar Street (demolished in the 1870s), 1859 to 1861
- 2 College Precincts, 1861 to 1863
- 10 High Street (demolished in the 1960s), 1863 to 1902

In the mid-1840s Ann was helping her sister, Elizabeth, to run the *Shades Tavern* at 16 Mealcheapen Street. When William Elgar came to Worcester to seek work in 1841, he stayed at the *Shades* and met Ann; they married in 1848. In 1842 William was appointed organist at St George's Roman Catholic Church in Sansome Place, shown on the map at the corner of Sansome Street and Sansome Fields Walk (now Sansome Walk); here Ann received religious instruction and was received into the Roman Catholic faith. (The authors are indebted to the research by the late K. E. L. & Marion Simmons for much of this information.)

5. Life at 10 High Street, 1863-1878 (first 15 years)

A double tragedy
Only a year after the Elgars' move to 10 High Street, tragedy struck: in 1864 Harry fell ill with scarlet fever. The worry concerning his health would have been immense for Ann. During the mid-1800s, pandemic outbreaks of scarlet fever in England caused a sharp rise in mortality. Four weeks after his attack of scarlet fever Harry died of chronic kidney disease at the age of only 15. Lucy remembered that 'this grief nearly cost my Father his reason, but by Mother's bravery and fortitude that awful calamity was averted'.[2] Ann was a tower of strength keeping the family going at that time.

We have the following moving passage in Lucy's 'Reflections'. Her mistake in putting Joe's death before Harry's does not affect the validity of what she is saying.

> (When) *after much suffering Joe passed away in the dawn of a September day in the 7th year of his age – it was a great grief – but consolation seemed to come under the calm resignation which Mother taught us.* (Then came) *the death of my brother Harry, after an illness of four weeks only. This grief nearly cost my Father his reason, but by Mother's bravery and fortitude that awful calamity was averted – At first it was an impossible sorrow, they did not, they could not, believe in it – why could such grief come to them? Life for them was empty, nothing but withered hopes – for on that first boy they had naturally built all their bright anticipations of the future … for they kept their trouble to themselves, helping and comforting each other in their daily tasks.*
>
> *She used to maintain: 'the laws of the body, its health and happiness, are as much God's laws as any other.'*

A little glimpse of what it cost Ann is given in the poem she copied into her scrapbook on 'Sorrow lightened by sun through a minster's stained glass window':

And methought as I gazed, that a lesson
From the storied pane did shine
And patience, and hope taught me
By a sorrow greater than mine.

Edward was now the eldest son.

Meanwhile the Elgar Brothers shop was thriving, no doubt dispelling some of the worries Ann may have had about the success of the new business. Ann would have had plenty to do, even with her two helpers, Kit the nurse, and Ned Spiers the general handyman – help that went beyond their nominal duties. Hubert Leicester left this illuminating memoir:

> *Ned Spiers, who had been stage carpenter with the touring companies, was their man who moved pianos and all the odd jobs. He met with an accident which left him with a limp but he was a tremendously strong man. He had seen all the great actors and quoted Shakespeare and speeches from all the repertory of the companies, and knew the whole of England, and was a wonderful companion – almost tutor to the children.*
>
> *'Kit' was the nurse and faithful servant of the family and came from Herefordshire. The family adored her, and her extraordinary misuse of words was their delight all their lives: many of her sayings became household words ...*[3]

Given that Edward was, in Hubert Leicester's words, 'always alive to every impression', we can easily imagine the broadly educative influence of these characters on both him and his mother.

Just over two years after Harry's death there was in 1866 the second tragedy already alluded to by Lucy. Little Joe, who was regarded as 'the Beethoven of the family', became unwell during the summer, and we can imagine Ann's anxiety as she attempted to restore his health but in vain, for he died of tuberculosis at seven. It does appear that, although he was so musically precocious, he was retarded in height and ability to pronounce words properly. He and Edward had been inseparable.

Two days after Joe was buried on 8 September 1866, his father – possibly as a distraction for Edward – managed to get him into a Three Choirs Festival rehearsal at the cathedral which was a truly stunning event in Edward's life. It was the first time he had heard an orchestra and he was ecstatic. According to notes left by Edward's daughter, Carice, following conversation with Hubert Leicester, he exclaimed: 'Oh my! I had no idea what a band was like. Then I began to think how much more could be made of it than they were making ...'[4]

Ann's interest in Edward's musical development

We believe that Ann was the more influential parent but acknowledge that William provided the musical background to Edward's childhood that must have guided him towards music as a profession. It could be said that Edward inherited musical interest and ability from his father and uncles and wider artistic sensitivity from his mother. It is significant that it was Ann, rather than his father, who showed an interest in Edward's early attempts at writing music. There appears to be a marked and inexplicable contrast in the attitude of Ann and

5. Life at 10 High Street, 1863-1878 (first 15 years)

William towards Edward. One would have expected William the musician to have delighted in his son's musical ability, but the anecdotes that have come down to us disprove this. Edward's friend Hubert Leicester recalled:

At 4 or 5 (Edward) was seen trying to write down a tune, drawing the lines himself on a plain sheet of paper and very puzzled because he could not get it right. His father, who was thought to be a gruff kind of man generally, said to him:
  'What are you doing there, you silly boy?'
  'Writing music,' was the reply.
  'Well, don't you know that music is written on five lines, not four?' was the father's comment ...[5]

As has been already mentioned, Ann – who was not naturally interested in music – seems to have recognised from the start Edward's special musical gifts. Hubert Leicester saw what was going on:

His mother was always ready to help and encourage him, but his father and uncle were merely amused and scoffed at his childish efforts – an attitude they persisted in until E. really had made his way in the world.[6]

William unwittingly provided an ideal environment for a young composer. The shop in itself was an education, with a vast variety of instruments and music, including scores of symphonies. The young Edward could browse here to his heart's content. Instead, however, of revelling in his son's wonderful interest in music, William appears to have been envious. An example occurred in 1869 when Edward, as a 'jape', inserted an additional little tune he had composed into rehearsal copies of Handel's *Messiah* to be used in the cathedral. Far from being delighted with this confident gesture, his father was furious, perhaps understandably. Apparently, the tune was well received by the musicians![7]

It remains surprising that William did not note and encourage the precocity of his son, especially when in one of the 'Worcester Papers' he had bewailed the fact that England had not produced any great composer!

On the other hand Ann seems not to have had much musical knowledge. Music is not mentioned much in the scrapbooks. (She has a passage on the violin, and she mentions the Swedish opera singer Jenny Lind at *Wynds Point*, Malvern.) It is significant, however, that she instinctively encouraged Edward's fascination with music and, when he acquired a copy of Reicha's *Orchestral Primer*, she inscribed in it 'Edward Elgar, March 7 1869.' Did Ann recognise the seeds of latent talent?

Back in 1866 she had copied what Edward had written on 24 March 1866: a pattern of two intersecting staves which, by using different clefs, allowed him to arrive at a single note at the centre to be interpreted simultaneously, in German notation, as B-A-C-H (Illust. 32). We refer to this later. Almost certainly Ann would not have understood the significance of this acrostic but recognised it as interesting and saved it.

Years later it transpired that she kept copies of all Edward's music manuscripts in a safe box, as she told his new friend Dr Charles Buck when introduced to him in 1881.[8] Buck had been impressed with Edward's *Air de Ballet* at a performance in Worcester at the fifth annual meeting of the British Medical Association in 1882 and he wanted to see a copy. Again Ann's ever-watchful presence in Edward's musical development was constructive.

She had already taken care of his education. In 1866, after attending Miss Walsh's Catholic Dame School at 11 Britannia Square, Edward went for a short time to a Catholic school run by nuns at *Spetchley Park* to the east of Worcester. (This required the nine-year-old to walk a daily round trip of five miles.)

In 1867 Ann enrolled Edward at his final school at *Littleton House* at Lower Wick on the south-western outskirts of Worcester. Here the master, Francis Reeve, won the respect and admiration of Edward and so was influential in his development. Reeve was not conventional in his approach to teaching and allowed Edward the freedom he needed to progress. Reeve's comment on the apostles resonated with Edward when, 30 years later, he embarked on his oratorio *The Apostles*:

> *The Apostles were young men and very poor. Perhaps, before the descent of the Holy Ghost, they were no cleverer than some of you here.*[9]

Ann was astute too in encouraging the friendship with Hubert Leicester, who was two years older than Edward. Together they would make their way to *Littleton House*, crossing the river by ferry. 'Wherever Hubert goes or whatever he does, you may join in,' she said to Edward, showing astonishing intuitive trust in the older boy (who would later become Mayor of Worcester).[10] Probably it was because Hubert was already a pupil at *Littleton House* and spoke highly of the teaching that Ann decided to send Edward there.

Ann and William must have discussed what Edward was to do when he left school at 15 in 1872. In spite of his clear musical talent and great interest in music, the music business was probably judged as too precarious, and the offer of being articled to a family solicitor friend, William Allen, clinched the matter. Edward applied himself well, but his heart was not in the law and, besides, he had

5. Life at 10 High Street, 1863-1878 (first 15 years)

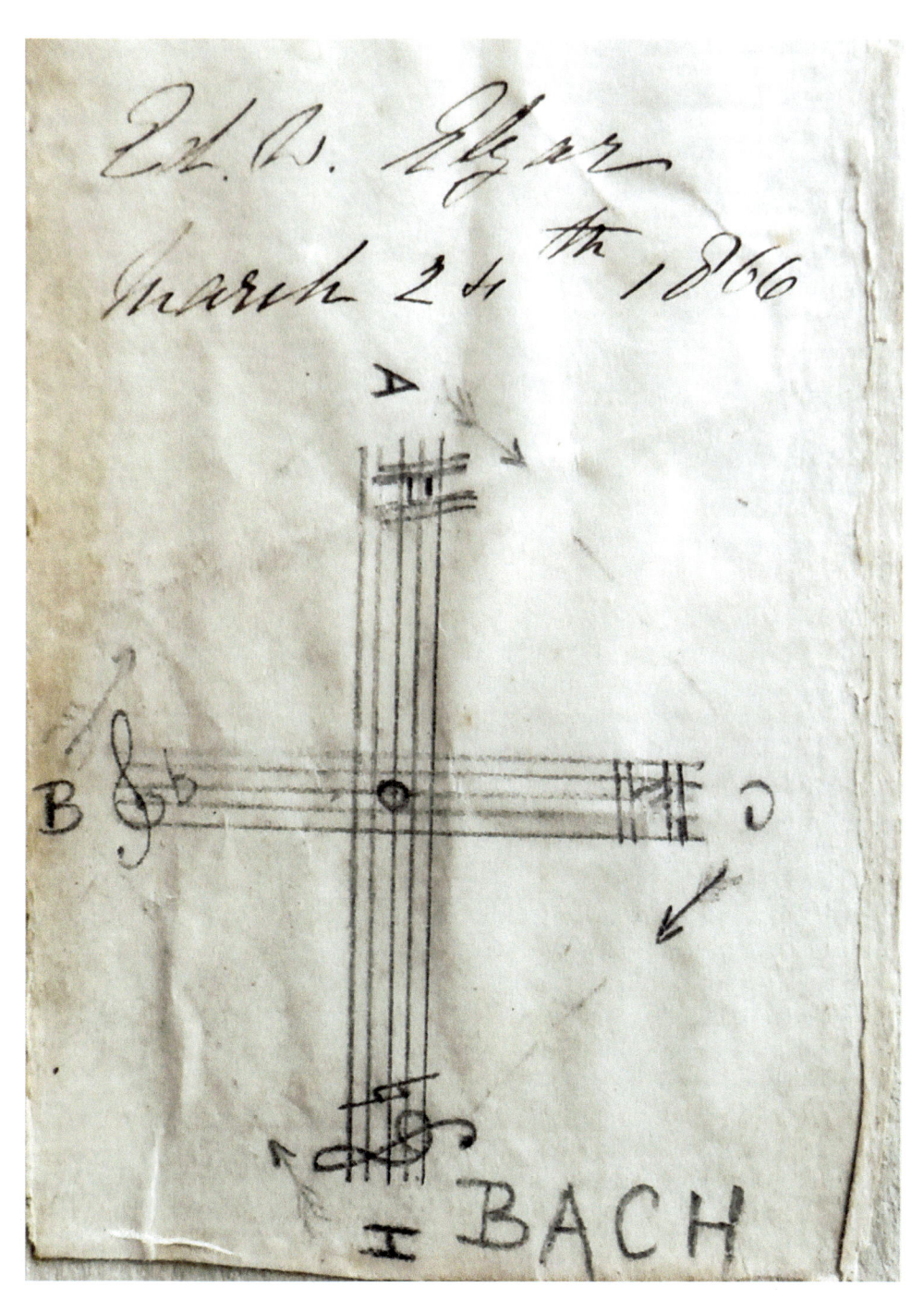

32. Cross-staves design on 'BACH' by Edward Elgar, 1866.

a rival in Allen's law firm who was making things difficult for him.[11] He told Sir Compton Mackenzie 50 years later that he discussed his aspirations with his mother (significantly, not his father).[12] After a year Edward resigned and started working in the family music business.

Illust. 33 shows Ann around 1870.

Ann's concern for all her children
It would be wrong to give the impression that Ann was not equally interested in the lives and activities of her other children, for she took the education of all of them seriously. The rhyming couplets about each of them, which she wrote in 1874, show her perceptiveness. While Edward's sensitivity was recognised:

Nervous, sensitive & kind
Displays no vulgar frame of mind.

Ann was equally concerned with his siblings. Lucy she saw as:

Dainty, little dainty girl
Fit to sit in gold or pearl.

When Lucy left home for a holiday in Paris on 23 May 1874, Ann wrote a special poem. The absence of Lucy for just a little while obviously meant a lot to her mother. Elgar biographer Jerrold Northrop Moore thinks this poem is too specific to be copied from anything else (scrapbook):

Thou art flown, my bird,
And my heart is stirred by sad emotion. All the day
Fly on to thy rest
In thy last year's nest.
I soon shall chirp my grief away,
For thine eye will be bright and plumage fine
In that fairer sunnier home than mine.

Of her three other surviving children Ann wrote the following lines. Pollie, who in later life was to be, along with Lucy, a staunch supporter of her mother, she described as:

Mirthful, saucy, singing lass
Greets you gaily as you pass.

5. Life at 10 High Street, 1863-1878 (first 15 years)

33. Photograph of Ann, c. 1870.

34. Photograph of the Elgar children, 1868.
(back row Edward & Pollie, front row Dot, Frank & Lucy).

5. Life at 10 High Street, 1863-1878 (first 15 years)

Pollie did indeed have a fine singing voice and sang solos. Frank Ann felt confident about:

As a graceful strong young tree
He will live on joyously.

Frank was to become an oboist and conductor of ensembles and eventually took on the running of the family music shop.

Dot, the youngest, seemed to her:

Slender, thoughtful, timid maid
Like a young fawn in the shade.

Dot, alone of her children, never married but was to have a very distinguished career, becoming Mother General of the Dominican nuns in Britain.

One interesting way in which Ann sought to cope with the loss of her two other children was by recording the development of the others in photography. All the Elgar children were regularly trooped into the photographer's studio; Illust. 34 shows them in 1868.

Box D: The Popularity of Longfellow in Victorian Society

All biographies of Elgar note his immersion in the thought of the American author Longfellow; it was Ann who nourished this interest in him. When she first came upon Longfellow's writings we do not know. He was born in 1807, but it was not until the 1860s that his work began to be widely known in England. Longfellow was the most-loved American poet of the nineteenth century. He was also one of the first writers to be able to support himself wholly by writing. Indeed, he was highly successful: by the 1870s he was earning the equivalent of 100,000 dollars a year. In England he outsold Tennyson and was the first American poet to be commemorated in Poets' Corner, Westminster Abbey.

Today it is fashionable to be somewhat dismissive of him both as a poet and novelist and for his ideas. This extract from a recent book on American literature puts this criticism into a proper historical perspective:

> *Viewed in relation to his own culture and his own poetic aspirations, Longfellow exhibited a metrical complexity, a mastery of sound and atmosphere, a progressive social conscience and a melancholy outlook for which his soothing words were especially appropriate, as though the poet were comforting himself as well as his audience.* (The Norton Anthology of American Literature, Vol.1, Beginnings to 1865, p.656.)

It is not surprising that Longfellow became almost a template for Ann's own outlook on life, as we can see in the following poem:

What the Heart of the Young Man Said to the Psalmist
(A Psalm of Life), **1839**

Tell me not in mournful numbers
Life is but an empty dream!
For the soul is dead that slumbers
And things are not what they seem

Life is real – life is earnest –
And the grave is not its goal
Dust thou art, to dust returnest
Was not spoken of the soul.

Not enjoyment, and not sorrow,
Is our destined end or way;
But to act, that each tomorrow
Find us further than today.

5. Life at 10 High Street, 1863-1878 (first 15 years)

Box D continued

In the world's broad field of battle
In the bivouac of Life.
Be not like dumb, driven cattle!
Be a hero in the strife!

Lives of great men all remind us
We can make our lives sublime
And, departing, leave behind us
Footsteps on the sands of time.

Footsteps that perhaps another
Sailing o'e life's solemn main,
A forlorn and shipwrecked brother
Seeing, shall take heart again.

Let us then be up and doing
With a heart for any fate,
Still achieving, still pursuing,
Learn to labour and to wait.

An interesting parallel between Longfellow and Elgar was their attitude to their birthplace. Longfellow never tired of praising his native city of Portland, Maine, where his birthplace has become a thriving museum. He wrote this poem about it:

From *My Lost Youth*, March 1855

Often I think of the beautiful town
That is seated by the sea;
Often in thought go up and down
The pleasant streets of that dear old town,
And my youth comes back to me,
And a verse of a Lapland song
Is haunting my memory still:
'A boy's will is the wind's will,
And the thoughts of youth are long, long thoughts.'

    How like Elgar's deep affection for Broadheath.
    It is just possible that Ann could have seen Longfellow, and we feel sure that she would in any case have read of his visit to Malvern in the summer of 1868.

Box D continued

Longfellow's association with Malvern

Longfellow was once a guest of glass manufacturer Edward Chance at *Lawnside*, a large house in Malvern that became a girls' school for well over a century. He planted a tree in the corner of a lawn.

The Malvern Advertiser in 1929 had a piece quoting an article by Canon James West of Leicester Cathedral, who began his career as a teacher in Malvern in 1866:

> *It must have been on his way south from the Lake District, before his visit to London and the Isle of Wight, that Longfellow stayed with Mr Edward Chance of Lawnside. I do not myself remember the date or even the month, but it was a bright summer day ... about the middle of July 1868. I was at that time a young master at the Preparatory School just opposite to Lawnside ... The boys and masters were invited to see Longfellow plant a tree in the beautiful grounds of Lawnside. I distinctly remember the features of the poet, venerable in appearance beyond his age. He struck me at the time as being nervous about the ceremony, and his sorrows had left their impress on his beautiful face.*
>
> *If any of the boys expected to hear him recite Excelsior, they were disappointed, but they listened with attention to the few words in which he expressed his pleasure in seeing them. To me personally it was a great joy when Miss Barrows recently showed me the tree, and I was especially interested to see that, after all these years, this memorial of the American Poet, full of life and strength, still adorns the garden at Lawnside.*

(Other eminent visitors to *Lawnside* were Lord Tennyson, G. K. Chesterton, George Bernard Shaw and Sir Edward Elgar. It was a girls' boarding school from the mid-nineteenth century till 1994, and its headmistress for many years was Miss Winifred Barrows, who was a friend of both Shaw and Elgar.)

5. Life at 10 High Street, 1863-1878 (first 15 years)

Ann's enduring love for the countryside

An utterly major characteristic of Ann was her affinity with the natural world. In her scrapbooks it is above all her love of nature that shines through. There are innumerable pictures of countryside, streams, birds, butterflies, plants, trees, flowers and country scenes, images of which are heard by many in Elgar's music. She has many comments about rivers, e.g., boating on the Severn and a paper on the age of the River Wye. She finished the second scrapbook with four extracts about ferns.

Ann's conviction of nature's recuperative power for us is clear in the following quotation from the 'Casket of Jewels' section in 'Worcester Papers':

Of all the tailors in the universe, there are none who can mend a hole in 'your coat' like dame Nature.

Lucy speaks of how soothing and comforting her mother found being in the open air:

She sought natural joy in her daily pinpricks by taking long walks, and commun(ing) with Nature in its beauty – when the air was sweet with the breath of violets and all the tender flowers of the first months of the year, when the sense of awakening is everywhere ... She loved an atmosphere peaceful yet glowing and vibrating with her own emotions.

Indeed in her scrapbook she included a verse from Coleridge[13] which beautifully sums up what nature meant to her:

With finest ministrations, thou, O Nature,
Healest thy wandering and distempered child.

Lucy notes that she and her mother had much in common: 'they would stroll side by side in the lanes, enjoying the quiet, and the beauty of the grasses and the flowers ...

'Here are some lines she sent me after one of our many wanderings.'
These refer to a picnic on the Old Hills (just south of Worcester) in June 1878:

Only a sprig of heather
But it grew upon the wild
Where you and I together
The summer day beguiled.

When the skylark high was singing
Above the yellow broom
And the cool hill-breeze was bringing
The sweet scent of its bloom.

The opportunities for excursions from Worcester into the surrounding countryside would not have been plentiful for Ann and her family, but we may be sure that, country-lover that she was, she would have taken as many as she could for the enlargement of her children's horizons and their health as well as for her own relaxation and delight. Victorians, moreover, were less averse to travelling by foot than their modern descendants. The limitations of the Elgars' excursions were probably determined much more by available free time than lack of motorised transport. Horse-drawn trips were certainly made to local beauty spots.

Ann never tired of thinking of the countryside, which they visited whenever possible. Here is an evocative poem written, we think, by Lucy about another outing to the Old Hills in July 1878.

Is it a tuft of bright thistle down
That came in the window and settled down?
Or is it the perfume of new-mown hay?
Something has roused my mother today.
She talks of a picnic of only three,
Gilda our guest, herself, and me.
Spiers must drive us, and Tip of course
Will run with Billy the old black horse,
The air is lovely, sunny and bright
Pa says there'll be a full moon tonight,
There's nothing to hinder a little spree
We're to go to the Wold Hills and get our tea,
And being Thursday we close at four,
The carriage will come and wait at the door.
It will not be more than a six mile drive,
We shall be there all right by five.
This was no sooner arranged than done,
Our faces all beaming over with fun.
We mounted and packed away our store
Of provisions, cloaks and wraps galore.

5. Life at 10 High Street, 1863-1878 (first 15 years)

Lucy recalled that Ann encouraged her children to go out in all weathers during the whole of the year. Jerrold Northrop Moore wrote that Ann 'did not fail to draw her children's attention to the congruence between the cycles of nature and a divinely ordered cycle'. He went on:

> *She used to send her children back to (the) countryside for summer holidays. In 1867 when Edward was 10, she sent him to stay with former neighbours at Broadheath. And there and then came the first scrap of dated music from his pen – a two-line 'Humoreske', subtitled 'a tune from Broadheath'. It was as though Broadheath had taught it to him.*[14]

Two years later the whole family stayed in the gardener's cottage in a grove of pines at *Spetchley Park*. This was very close to the Catholic school to which Edward had trudged daily. Once again the countryside was to inspire him. When in 1900 he set to music John Henry Newman's poem *The Dream of Gerontius*, the phrase 'the lofty pines' vividly brought back to him the pines at Spetchley. Truly, Ann's passionate love for the countryside was woven into the very texture of Edward's music.

6.
Later Years in Worcester, 1878-1902

In 1879 the Elgar family began to leave home. Pollie was the first to go: on St George's Day she married William Grafton, and Ann wrote a special poem for them. The couple moved into 35 Chestnut Walk (now 12 Sansome Walk), not far from the Catholic church. Before the year was out Edward went to live with them in a bedroom at the top of the house.

Ann was clearly delighted in the following year at the birth of her first grandchild. In her scrapbook there is a touching reference to 'my angel May born 10 mins. before 2 o'clock Sun May 23 1880'. This surely suggests that Ann was in the house at the time. She was careful to note the birthdays of Pollie and Will's other three children too.

The following year Lucy married Charles Pipe, to whom she had been engaged for some time. Ann had been unhappy about the marriage, because Charlie was not a Catholic. So on 15 August 1880 he resolved the issue by being received into the Catholic Church, possibly just to appease Ann. He and Edward seem to have been good friends, for soon afterwards they both went to Paris, a city Charlie knew well.

Frank, the younger surviving son, left home in 1889 when he married Mary Agnes Bamford, and they lived across the River Severn in Henwick, where they had three children. Ann must have seen more of him, as he had taken over the running of the family firm.

Meanwhile, Ann kept in close touch with her brother, John, in America. Sadly, however, hardly any of their extensive correspondence has survived. We do know that for John's birthday on 14 September 1882 she sent his son Charles photographs of her children together with a poem, *Aunty's Picture of the Jewels*, explaining why there were two children missing from the photographs:

Aunty's picture of the jewels
In her earthly diadem:
Two have been removed for safety,
So she cannot send them.

6. Later Years in Worcester, 1878-1902

If perchance across the surface
Shines a ray of lustre bright,
Think it's a bit of radiance
From the others out of sight.

Ann's family meant an enormous amount to her. There are many references in her scrapbook to the Greening family, including a society wedding in Mayfair of Miss Amelia Greening and a long extract in her own handwriting, copied from a tomb in Newnham-on-Severn Churchyard by William Elgar on 8 September 1879, about Christopher Greening and the manufacture of needles, first made in England in the mid-sixteenth century.

In 1876 Ann had reflected on her time as a mother and wrote her very personal thoughts about it in her scrapbook. She is being acutely honest here in her reaction to the extraordinary changes towards the upbringing of children in her lifetime:

It is no joke to have five men and women to rule, and keep peace between, and to keep home in some order and comfort. With so many dispositions, different ways and wants, each one wrestling for the mastery – or trying to have their own way in defiance of the rest. Yes! I own it at last. I have given them too much latitude. I have ruled by love instead of terror and the fetters are too weak for their stronger passions. I failed to see that they could be different to myself, forgetting I was alone in my youth for so many years, I had no-one to disobey, to quarrel with or to play with, but my parents to whom I always gave implicit, blind obedience, I never remember stopping to question their authority or their wisdom – hence, I suppose I expect too much – but I should be happier if they were a little more like I was.

The scrapbook gives another very interesting insight into her inner thoughts which reveals much about her character and how she had to work on herself:

I have found nearly all my life (when in health) that change of occupation is varied, rests both the mind and body as completely as doing nothing. But after the age of 52 I find the body requires more entire cessation from all exertion, the elasticity is in a measure gone, the will is good as ever but the power less. There **must** *be times of perfect rest, from all mental as well as bodily fatigue that change will not bring. This is my experience. 1874.*

Lucy can describe her as serene and happy and even asked whether she had any cares, but these passages show she had to work hard to achieve that serenity and happiness – it was not just a sunny disposition. We know in any case that her life was far from easy, bringing up seven children with only modest financial means. Moreover, she had the anguish of losing Harry and Joe.

Ann was fond of aphorisms and on 6 January 1878 pasted this into her scrapbook:

We live in deeds not years, in thoughts not breaths; in feelings not in figures on a dial. We should count time by heart-throbs. He most lives who thinks most, feels the noblest, acts the best. Jan 6 1878.

Ann's awareness of Edward's genius
Although we have noted that Ann was not particularly musical, she nonetheless followed Edward's career in her scrapbooks, and it was noted and occasionally referenced in her writings. Here are a few items:

- An advertisement for a teaching post from *The Tablet*.
- A very detailed report of a concert by the Worcester Amateur Instrumental Society, in which 'Mr Elgar's *Air de Ballet*, and his new march *Pas Redoublé*' were much applauded. (Clearly Ann was keeping an eye on the press for her not-yet-famous son.)
- An advert regarding Edward's career, June 1878.
- Tickets for three concerts suggest that Ann herself attended these: a Worcester Amateur Instrumentalist Society concert at the Guildhall, conducted by Edward. (This was a concert with a good audience, at which Edward should have played a violin solo but he had injured a finger.) On 13 December 1883, a concert in Birmingham at which Edward's *Intermezzo* was performed by Stockley's orchestra, in which Edward played first violin and, on 5 February 1884, his *Sevillaña*.
- A hand-written note of 1884 that Edward's *Sevillaña* was performed at the Crystal Palace.
- A concert in which Edward conducted the Worcester Amateur Instrumental Society on 9 April in the Public Hall, Worcester: 'Under the careful and competent direction of Mr Edward Elgar the various pieces in the programme were performed with excellent affect.' The main work was Schubert's *Unfinished Symphony*, 'but the most enthusiastic display of the evening was called forth by a composition from the pen of Mr. Elgar, the talented conductor of the society, entitled *Sevillaña*.'
- On 10 September 1891 William Stockley conducted Edward's *Froissart* – a detailed report was given which included the comment: 'the overture would gain from compression, but enthusiastically received'.

6. Later Years in Worcester, 1878-1902

How thrilling it must have been for Ann to see him becoming noticed. There are no further references to Edward's career, probably because by now he was married and had moved to London.

Edward left the family home in 1879 when he took up residence in Pollie and Will's house. We cannot be surprised at this. Edward was now 22 years old and struggling to make his way as a musician; he clearly needed both independence and freedom from the distraction of living with the family above the shop. Illust. 35 shows Edward at about this time.

When the Graftons moved house to Stoke Prior near Bromsgrove later in 1883, so that Will could be nearer his work, Edward did not return to live above the shop but went to live with Lucy and Charlie at 4 Field Terrace, off the Bath Road in Worcester. He was to stay for six years until his own marriage.

This was not a happy period for Edward, as he saw first his great friends Hubert Leicester and Charles Buck married, then his younger brother, Frank, become engaged, whilst his own engagement in the summer of 1883 to Helen Weaver came to an end in 1884.

Little is known as to why Helen pulled out of the attachment. There may have been religious grounds involved, as Helen's family were Protestant chapel-goers. Ann appears, however, to have got on well with the Weavers. She travelled up with Helen to attend the concert in Birmingham held on 13 December 1883, at which Edward's *Intermezzo Moresque* was performed by William Stockley's Orchestra, in which Edward played first violin.

Meanwhile, Edward was having to support himself teaching – an occupation he did not greatly enjoy. However, one of his piano-accompaniment pupils attracted his attention. She was Caroline Alice Roberts, who belonged to the minor aristocracy: her father was the late Major General Sir Henry Roberts of the Indian Army. It rapidly became clear that the attraction was mutual.

We wonder what Ann's reaction was when Edward became engaged to Alice in 1888. She is likely to have felt in some awe at Alice's social status. Would she, in her humble role as wife of a tradesman, be able to feel comfortable in the presence of a lady whose father had had a distinguished career in India? Class differences were still very pronounced in late Victorian society. She may have been surprised that Alice was a much older woman – nine years older than Edward. We suspect Ann may have been disappointed once again that the fiancée was not a Catholic. (Alice was to be received into the Roman Catholic Church several years after her marriage.)

We have no record of the qualms she almost certainly had, quite apart from the special trauma which can attend a mother seeing her son married. It is possible that Ann was worried about the future of her own close relationship with Edward.

35. *Photograph by Vanderweyde of Edward Elgar at 21.*

6. Later Years in Worcester, 1878-1902

There was strong disapproval of the marriage from many of Alice's relations, so the wedding took place in London in 1889 in as quiet a manner as possible. Only Pollie and Henry Elgar represented the Elgars, and one of Lucy's friends. Unlike Ann's own wedding in London, the reasons for this were all too obvious. It was a socially awkward arrangement, to say the least. We should remember that Roman Catholicism in late nineteenth-century Britain was still regarded with some suspicion by many on political, religious and social grounds.

Ann wrote to Edward:

One little word of heartfelt congratulations on your marriage day & happy union to my darling boy. May you have many happy years together – luxuriating in joy, love, & goodness as each year rolls along – And my hearty prayers will be always, God Bless you.

A ribbon from Alice's bouquet was sent to Ann after the ceremony, a kind thought.

In her scrapbook Ann included a map of the Isle of Wight, where Edward and Alice spent their honeymoon, and marked on the two places where they stayed. She also pasted in one of Alice's printed poems which were under the name of Caroline R., entitled *Question and Answer*:

What is our life? The floating of a feather
Adown the wavy current of the breeze;
A blossom fading in the summer weather,
A dead leaf falling from the forest trees;
A bubble breaking in the wind's soft kiss?
Not this! Not this!

Later that year Edward and Alice took temporary residence at *Saetermo* in The Lees in Malvern, an area Alice had lived in earlier. Ann sent them flowers as a welcome, and a few days later paid them an afternoon visit. But Alice did not very often visit the Elgars in their music shop. Alice had grown up with very rigid ideas of class and so must have found adjusting to many of Edward's friends difficult.

In time Alice and Ann came to respect each other, even with a degree of affection. So it happened that Ann was invited to stay overnight before Alice and Edward returned to London. The next afternoon Ann and Edward went for a long walk together. This was probably an important moment for both of them, an opportunity to explore how each other felt about Alice's entry into the Elgar family.

When the lease at *Saetermo* expired, Edward and Alice found a house in London, whose music publishers and concert halls seemed to offer a better chance of furthering Edward's career as a composer. When in 1890 Edward came back to Worcester to play violin in a Herefordshire Philharmonic concert on 9 April, he stayed with his parents. Later that year Ann received an ecstatic postcard from Edward, written on 8 August, because Novello had accepted for publication his overture *Froissart*. Six days later Carice was born, and on 1 September 1890 both grandparents went to London to see the new grandchild, and Ann attended her christening on the following day. There is a story to this: Edward wrote to Dot on 26 August that he wished mother and father had been coming to the christening but 'I did not say much to mother in the way of regret as I thought it might make her more sorry she did not come.'[1]

We can imagine the discussion which took place in the Elgar household as Dot conveyed to Ann how much Edward wanted her to go. The then anti-Catholic William would not attend the ceremony, of course, but he did join the party for luncheon afterwards.

Ann was clearly delighted at Carice's birth and later wrote loving letters to her. See Illust. 36 and 37 for a facsimile of a delightful letter she wrote on 5 March 1897. She writes to her granddaughter with real affection and interest in the mind of a seven-year-old. Her enthusiasm for books shines through. The pressed flower at the top of the letter is typical of her.

The first few years of Edward's new life as a married man were spent in London, and, when he and Alice returned to Worcestershire in 1891, it was not Worcester but Malvern where they settled. There was less opportunity for Ann to see her son, but he always remembered to send her numerous postcards from his holidays.

In his comprehensive biography of Edward, Jerrold Northrop Moore makes an interesting comment for the year 1879: 'For the ageing mother pursuing her family duties at 10 High Street, the creative urge that formerly made a special bond with Edward had taken the son where the mother could not follow.'[2] This points to an undoubtedly wistful experience for Ann – quite unavoidable but something with which she felt she had to come to terms. Characteristically, she did so by composing a poem beginning:

Into the belfry tower one night
My wandering fancy winged
For the dear voices of the night
Had lured me with their spell…
Saying 'Why come here to see
The secrets of our minstrelsy?'

6. Later Years in Worcester, 1878-1902

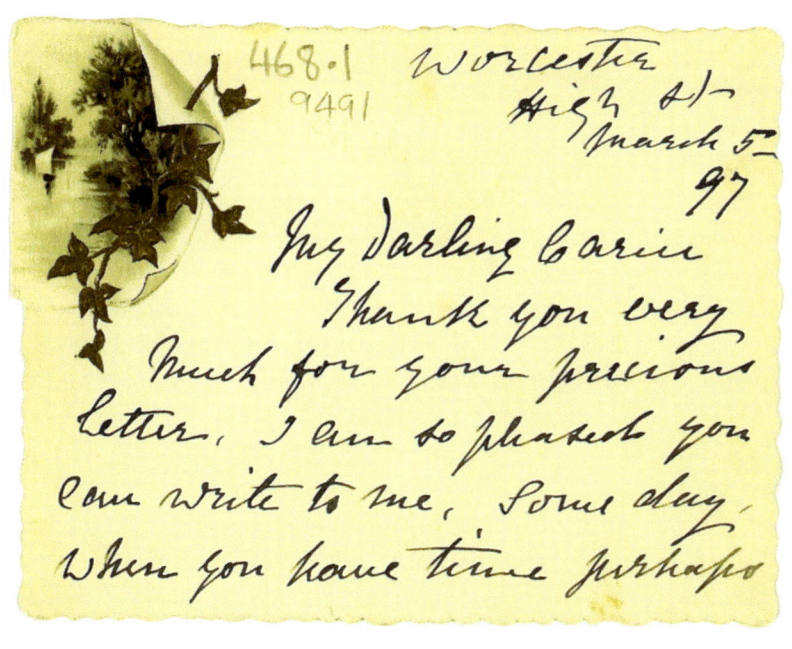

> 468·1
> 9491
>
> Worcester
> High St
> March 5
> 97
>
> My darling Carice
>
> Thank you very much for your precious letter, I am so pleased you can write to me. Some day, when you have time perhaps

36. Facsimile of letter (page 1) from Ann to her granddaughter Carice on 5 March 1897.

> you will tell me the names of your five dolls, and if they are pretty,
> I am glad you have a book you like, to read, and that tells you about nice people
> with love and a kiss, my sweet darling. ever your affectionate
> Grandmama
> A. Elgar

37. Facsimile of letter (page 2) from Ann to her granddaughter Carice on 5 March 1897.

These were the secrets of little goblins striking the bells 'with precision and wonderful power' which, it transpired, could not be revealed:

I cough'd, and I hemme'd but no word could I say
And saw the last little one turning away
When there came a loud knocking! Dot opened the door!
Saying 'Ma, you sleep soundly, I've called you before!

In July and August 1892 Edward and Alice began their tour of Germany and they sent Ann nine postcards. They visited Beethoven's birthplace in Bonn and saw Wagner's *Parsifal* in Bayreuth. Edward sent a special postcard to his mother from Heidelberg:

Dearest Mother,
I must send a line from here about which we have read & thought so much. I have marked with a cross our hotel which is above the Castle: it is exquisitely lovely here & we are just going exploring. Last night we accomplished a good slice of home journey – Lindau to Heidelberg – you will see on your map: then when driving up here we suddenly had to stop & make way for a great procession of Students – torch-light – the three duelling guilds with a brass band & marching – all their faces wounded (silly fools) & many with bandages on – gay uniforms & no end of torches: it did remind me of Hyperion & the beer scandal &c. &c.

The following year they visited Garmisch, where they stayed at the *Villa Bader* with friends of Alice. Again they sent cards to Ann, 14 altogether. They clearly wanted to share their experiences with her. Here is an example, 9 August 1893 from Garmisch:

Here are A & myself sitting in the forester's house half way up a mountain (just as you see above) & saying how Mother wd. like all this. Blue sky, fir trees, waterfalls, grass hoppers singing loudly & bright sunshine. Much love to all. EE & CAE.

During 1895 they journeyed from Bruges to Austria via the Danube. This time they sent Ann 21 cards. Edward sent a long letter to his mother from Bruges, where they were staying with friends of Alice in 'a large sort of chateau-house' close by:

This house has a large sort of arrangement of (illegible) *doors and mirrors (?) hall with a marble floor – rooms so lofty & the house full of old furniture & brass fittings & pottery wd. send you wild. ghostly though & by their light I skip through the corridors nimbly. It's a beautiful house though.*

Edward knew that Ann would share his interest in architecture and furnishing. He was clearly enjoying himself:

There is a golf ground here and I have been playing a good deal & I am considered a great player & have been coaching some of the men – such fun!

A shorter holiday in 1897 to Cologne and Garmisch still produced four cards to Ann, despite the fact that Edward was now beginning to be famous.

Ann's understanding of Edward's genius

There are many hints in the scrapbooks of Ann's awareness of Edward's genius. Is this Ann seeking to understand her son? The lengthy hand-written extract from Longfellow's *Hyperion* on genius from 2 October 1876 comes right at the beginning. *Hyperion* embodies the thoughts of a young fictional American, Paul Flemming, as he travels through Germany. The conversation which especially appealed to Ann was from Chapter VII, 'Lives of Scholars', and Chapter VIII, 'Literary Fame'. The extract she gives covers four points: how sensitive and temperamental such persons are allowed to be; that the main motivation for them should not be seeking fame but doing their duty – using conscientiously the gifts given; that genius is beyond not just their own age but all ages; and that genius is prone to great suffering which can, as it were, sanctify them.

Edward's ambition to be recognised as a composer was realised after the success of his cantata *Scenes from the Saga of King Olaf* in October 1896. For his mother this was a time of indescribable joy. She wrote to Edward himself:

My dearest boy,
    How the world is singing with high praise of your worth – Alice dear, what a proud wife you are – I can find no words to express a hundredth part of what I feel & dad & Lucy came home safely, & never expected to have had so much pleasure & joy – Bennett* has surpassed himself. I like his report Best.
    Ever your loving mother.

* Music critic Joseph Bennett in *The Daily Telegraph*.

To Alice she wrote the day after:

High Street Worcester
Sunday Novr 1st (1896)
My dearest Alice
   Thank you very much for the dear little letter today. I have lived in a dream for the last few days – I need not say take care of the precious boy (and yourself too) – no words of mine are equal to the occasion – I am deeply & truly thankful for all has been so very sweet and charming, always thanking you, dear, I am yours affect'ly
A. Elgar[3]

On the reverse side she wrote this poem:

To my boy
I will not praise as others praise –
   Thou needs it not from me,
The Genius has won its mead,
   And fame is crowning thee.
I care not that my life should tell
   What every life tells o'er.
The grandest spirit owns thy spell
   And mine can do no more.

King Olaf

Ann's influence on Elgar regarding spiritual insight could be seen in an interesting way in a lecture given by Professor John T. Hamilton on 'Cross against Corselet: Elgar, Longfellow, and the Saga of King Olaf'.[4] The performance of *King Olaf* in 1896 played a very important part in the development of Elgar's career. Interestingly, in 1924 he told his friend Troyte Griffith 'If I had to set K.O. again I shd. do it just in the same way …'[5]

A hidden thread linking these themes is provided by Ann. Firstly, the *King Olaf* theme comes from Longfellow's writings. Ann was the one who so enthusiastically introduced Longfellow to Elgar. See Box D, The Popularity of Longfellow in Victorian Society. His passion for Longfellow continued throughout his life. When in 1931 he wanted to give something very special to Vera Hockman, he gave her 'a little book – Longfellow's *Hyperion* – which for many years belonged to my mother; since then it has gone with me everywhere. I want you to have it because you are my mother, my child, my lover and my friend.'[6]

6. Later Years in Worcester, 1878-1902

Secondly, this had a fascinating precursor. Hamilton comments:

This fourfold identification of the young muse ... reflects a persistent pattern in Elgar's thinking, a pattern which reaches back to one of the earliest and most intriguing documents we have of the composer's youth. On a sheet dated March 24 1866 eight-year-old Elgar inscribed two intersecting staffs and, by employing different clefs and time signatures, allowed the single note at the centre to be interpreted simultaneously, in German notation, as B-A-C-H.

He notes further:

With remarkable acuity, the young Elgar employed the cross to reveal how Johann Sebastian Bach, who lived and worked during a particular historical period, can also be understood as a timeless master, who transcends any determinate time.

We owe the survival of this document to Ann's specific copy of it.

Thirdly, the subject-matter and the acrostic are not all that shows Ann's influence. Hamilton continues:

The richly complex symbolism of the Christian cross would not have been lost on Elgar, who was raised in his mother's Roman Catholicism. The cross's vast network of meaning proceeds from its foundational gambit: the cross is simultaneously a sign of death and a sign of everlasting life.

How to hold apparently contradictory ideas together requires an openness of mind for which Ann was again important. She shared in the fascination for Norse mythology which caught hold in Europe and America during the nineteenth century yet without the commonly-held understanding of it as replacing Christianity. It was fashionable in many quarters to regard the Christian tradition as weak and anaemic by comparison with Nordic heathenism, which was, as Hamilton put it, 'valiant, technologically innovative, and unabashedly passionate'.

The contrast between the impact of Norse mythology on Wagner and on Elgar is marked. Wagner stays with Thor's view of its supremacy:

Force ruled the world still,
Has ruled it, shall rule it,
Meekness is weakness,
Strength triumphant.

Elgar finishes with a note of victory for the Christian approach:

Cross against corselet,
Love against hatred,
Peace-cry for war-cry!
Patience is powerful.
He that o'ercometh
Hath power o'er the nations!

Elgar, though deeply immersed like Wagner in Norse mythology, retained his own approach to its interpretation. We do not think it is mere speculation to see here once again his mother's influence.

A very obvious instance of Ann's continuing influence on Edward concerns the composition of his cantata *Caractacus*. In a letter to her daughter Pollie dated 11 December 1898 she describes how she had been staying at Colwall, where Edward had visited her. 'I said "Oh Ed! Look at the lovely old hill, can't we write some tale about it?" "Do it yourself, Mother." He held my hand with a firm grip. "Do," he said. "No, I can't, my day is gone if ever I could," and so we parted – and in less than a month he told me *Caractacus* was all cut and dried and he had begun to work at it.'[7]

(Caractacus, properly Caratacus, was a first-century British chieftain who fought against the Roman conquest of Britain. One legend places his last stand at The British Camp on the Malvern Hills, although historians now doubt this. After his defeat, he was taken to Rome and allowed to speak to the Roman senators, who were so impressed by his nobility that he was allowed to live in peace in Rome.)

The conversation at Colwall took place when Ann was 76: perhaps it is not surprising she felt the way she did. What is interesting is the belief in his mother's creative capacity which Edward still showed. Sometime later on, when talking to a close friend, Ann revealed how Edward had, after the successful performance of *King Olaf* in 1896, come to see her, 'put his head in her lap and said he could not face the exposure'.[8]

The fact that Ann was quite out of her depth with regard to the music he was writing did not alter his faith in her general judgement. After the publication of the *Enigma Variations* (*Variations on an Original Theme (Enigma)*) in 1899 she wrote to Alice:

The dear boy's variations have come today – of course, no one could play or understand them – I shall live in hopes of hearing him play them some day –

Bless him and his works ... I feel a bit like a slipper boy's mother* – mother will sit at the door and pray – all I can do – give him my love and blessings.

* The allusion is lost on the authors.

Ann presented a remarkable and encouraging role model for Edward. She did not teach him as such but, by example, encouraged that confidence and enthusiasm for learning which was so distinctive of him. It enabled him to turn what otherwise might have been seen as a distinct disadvantage in the lack of high-level music education to the creation of his own very individual style.

Would Edward have 'dabbled' sufficiently in chemistry to carry out experiments in his shed ('The Ark' at his home *Plas Gwyn* in Hereford), designed a novel piece of chemistry equipment that went into commercial manufacture (the 'Elgar Sulphuretted Hydrogen Apparatus'), and studied diatoms under the microscope (at *Severn House* in Hampstead) without being enthused by her in the world and life at large? We think not. (Elgar's contemporary Hubert Parry had a similar interest in science, using a microscope to study fungi and algae.)

Fiftieth wedding anniversary

In January 1898 Ann and William celebrated their Golden Wedding Anniversary. Lucy records how it took place 'in the midst of their family, and under the most happy and pleasant associations, and a photograph, taken during the same week, gives the real expression of happiness on their dear old faces.' (See Illust. 38.) The following notice appeared in the local paper *Berrow's Worcester Journal*. Charlie Pipe, Lucy's husband, recalled:

> *They had no family gathering as they were not well enough, but all their relations who lived near called some time of the day and congratulated them. Letters they had galore, and amongst the numerous visitors they were not forgotten by Lord and Lady Alwyne Compton, the Lord Bishop of Ely and his Lady.*

(Lord Compton had been Dean of Worcester before moving to Ely, and his wife had contributed to the musical life of Worcester.)

Visit of Charles Greening

Ann's older brother, John, died on 22 February 1900, aged 84. His son Charles Greening then made the long journey from America with his wife, Clara, to visit the family in Worcester. As Clara wrote later in her autobiography, recalling her

38. Photograph of Ann & William Elgar, c.1900.
This was probably taken in the garden of 10 High Street by Ann's granddaughter May Grafton. Atypical of Victorian photographs, it is not posed but shows the pair momentarily distracted from their domestic chores. Ann, in her late 70s, sits outside a greenhouse, doing some sewing, and William, of similar age, stands alongside in gloves with scissors or secateurs in hand.

first visit to her future in-laws: 'We had some very jolly times and his people were very kind to me.'

When they reached 10 High Street, Worcester, it was such a memorable occasion for them all. Charles and his brother James had served in the American Civil War on the side of the Union. He had trained as a tinsmith and opened a hardware store and then a bank in Minnesota.[9] Charles later wrote the following, which is contained in Lucy's 'Reflections':

> *Never shall I forget the hearty welcome given the Yankee Nephew by his English Aunt. The kindly loving expression on her face well repaid me for the long journey and verified my father's pride in his favourite sister's splendid disposition and character.*
>
> *The highest tribute I can pay her memory is this; she was one of God's good women.*[10]

Edward's acclaim for *The Dream of Gerontius*

We have written of Ann's reaction to Edward's success with his works *King Olaf* and the *Enigma Variations*. A work was to follow, a setting of John Henry Newman's poem *The Dream of Gerontius*, that, after a shaky premiere in Birmingham in 1900 but a wildly successful performance in Germany the following year, secured the composer's international fame. Michael Kennedy calls *The Dream of Gerontius* Elgar's finest work and describes the effect of this success upon Ann and her gifted son:

> *After the second Düsseldorf* Dream of Gerontius, *Alice wrote an account of the performance and of (Richard) Strauss's tribute for her mother-in-law. In her reply from the music shop home Ann wrote 'What can I say to him the dear one. I feel that he is some great historic person – I cannot claim a little bit of him now he belongs to the big world.'*[11]

Kennedy points out the irony in Ann's tribute, for Ted Elgar of Worcester was becoming increasingly conflicted by his rapid elevation as an historical personage both at home and abroad:

> *Though his creations were his private kingdom, Elgar was constitutionally unable to seal them off from other facets of his mind.*

Ann witnessed this conflict, but what could she do apart from listen and support in the few months of life left to her?

Ann's death
Ann became frail in her late seventies and, after her 80th birthday in 1902, her health deteriorated markedly. Lucy, in her 'Reflections', recorded on Monday 1 September:

Dear Mother! She was fully conscious that she soon must leave the beautiful world she had so loved, for a realm which was to her only 'an undiscovered country' – and in our quiet talks together, towards the end, she would clasp my hand and say, 'I often wonder what it will be like' – sometimes I could scarcely answer for the choking tears – and made an excuse to turn aside, so as not to distress her – at other times words came, and I said all I could to comfort, and to make easy the journey that was soon coming. I often felt a poor thing, and very incapable of saying things as I thought then, and wanted to convey my meaning, but I did my best.

A friend of Edward's, Rosa Burley, recorded that he visited her that day and was much affected:

… (Edward) was so deeply moved that he could hardly speak, for he knew that she was dying. I have always regretted that I was never allowed to meet old Mrs Elgar since there is no doubt that she was the best influence he ever knew. To her training he owed many of his best qualities and I think it is true to say that the first bitterness of losing her coincided in his case with the beginnings of that Weltschmerz *from which every artist seems to suffer when he has achieved what he believes to be the summit of his success.*[12]

Ann died that day from heart failure.[13] Dot was with her at the end. Alice wrote in her diary: 'E's dear Mother passed away most peacefully in the morning.' Ann was buried three days later at Worcester's Astwood Cemetery beside her two sons Harry and Joe. She had done well to reach 80: in 1841, 19 years after her birth, the average newborn girl was not expected to see her 43rd birthday. William lived on to 84, when he too died of heart failure,[14] and was buried with her. Life expectancy in 1900 was 44 for males, so William also did well. In 1996 a headstone was erected by the Elgar Society, the Elgar family and the Elgar Foundation (Illust. 39).

The *Worcester Herald* reported on 6 September 1902 a Three Choirs rehearsal on 1 September in Worcester Guildhall of *The Dream of Gerontius*, conducted by Edward:

6. Later Years in Worcester, 1878-1902

39. *Elgar family grave (including Ann), Astwood Cemetery, Worcester.*

In the course of the rehearsal Dr Elgar informed the choir that his mother had passed away that day. One of her last words to him, he added, was to express the wish that he would not allow her death to interfere with any of his engagements.

The following week Edward conducted a truly memorable performance of the work. The composer Granville Bantock wrote to the music critic Ernest Newman (whose real name was William Roberts) in the most ecstatic terms possible about the performance:

Believe me, my dear Will, although Elgar & I look at music through different spectacles, his Gerontius is beyond all criticism or cavil. It is a great, great work, & the man who wrote it is a Master, and a Leader. We were all deeply affected, and gave way to our feelings. While Elgar was conducting, the tears were running down his cheeks. I want to hear nothing better. I have felt as if transfixed by a spike from the crown of my head to my feet. Once on hearing Parsifal at Bayreuth, when the dead swan is brought on, & today, at the words 'Novissima hora'.[15]

The *Westminster Gazette* printed the following:

Queens of Sheba in great numbers, their regalia and best hat and a netted bag of sandwiches and octavo scores, came this morning to hear the wonders of King Elgar's wisdom ... The Cathedral is said to seat three thousand ... persons, and there were some who had to stand. By popular acclaim, Mr Elgar has certainly been crowned.

There is no question in our minds that Ann would have been greatly amused to read this.

7.
Ann's Influence on Edward

The reason we have written this book is to articulate why Ann was so important for Edward's life and career. We feel that her input is mostly either taken for granted or underestimated in light of the enormous amount of information about her son's later life and the huge number of other sources of inspiration for him.

Firstly, we shall look at what Elgar's biographers have said about her. The views range from the first biography of Elgar, with a highly eulogistic passage, to a comment by others, such as Diana McVeagh, to a thoughtful perception by David Nice, to Michael Kennedy and Percy Young, who pay deeper tribute to her influence. A less sympathetic portrayal by Michael De-la-Noy follows before concluding with Jerrold Northrop Moore, who is convinced that Ann provided the essential basis for Edward's genius to emerge.

R. J. Buckley, Elgar's first biographer, writes:

> ... she read translations of Latin classics, of the Greek tragedians, and talked in the home of what she read. 'The best woman that ever drew breath' is the description of one who knew her for a lifetime, and this testimony of a non-relative is confirmed on every hand. Blessed are they who have mothers like the mother of Edward Elgar![1]

Diana McVeagh's brief assessment:

> Elgar's mother died in 1902. She had instilled his ideals, and had peopled his mind with 'heroes and poets'.[2]

David Nice:

> There can be no doubt that Elgar loved her dearly. She communicated to him something of her intense feeling for nature – the Blakean ability 'to see a World in a Grain of Sand/And a Heaven in a Wild Flower' – and her conviction that one must 'be always busy, doing something that is useful and interesting.' Prone to verse-making of her own, she was well read.[3]

> *The tenacity of Edward's mother in her intellectual pursuits seems all the more remarkable given the constant demands of her seven children.*[4]

Michael Kennedy:

> *When his mother died in the late summer of 1902 (Edward) lost the first moulding influence on his mind, for it was she who had stimulated his love of literature and the world of nature around him. Although, like all children, he had sometimes felt misunderstood by his parents, Elgar had an abiding love and respect for the 'two honest burghers' as he called them to Troyte Griffith.*[5]

Percy Young echoes that:

> *She was indefatigable – cheerfully controlling a large and lively family on slender means yet pursuing her private interest at the same time.*[6]
> *Her death immediately removed a great source of inspiration.*[7]

It is fascinating to consider two particularly different portrayals of Ann. Michael De-la-Noy speaks of:

> *... her 'home-spun accomplishments ... she never strove to appear more clever than she was, and her verses and the tight little pencil sketches she drew were modest, effective tributes to her own small talent and sympathetic nature ... In so far as it is possible to piece together anything like a comprehensive picture of Ann from the fragments of evidence, including photographs, one gets the impression of a simple, kindly woman drawing comfort from religion, content with her role in life and sensitive to the aims and potential of others.*[8]

De-la-Noy goes on:

> *Far from coming to love the world, in many ways Elgar came to hate it. Why this was no one will ever know for certain, but on the assumption that the characteristics of most of our adult behaviour are formed in childhood, it is reasonable to deduce that Elgar's early years were not entirely happy.*[9]

The assessment of Ann as a 'simple' woman with 'small talent' differs markedly from that of Elgar's most assiduous biographer, Jerrold Northrop Moore, who sees the warm, inspiring and enquiring spirit of Ann as the catalyst nurturing his genius:

7. Ann's Influence on Edward

Her intellectual curiosity, honesty, and persistent encouragement were decisive factors in forming Edward's creative genius.[10]

The wonderful start in life, which he received at Broadheath in his first two years, gave him the confidence and ambition to pursue life energetically, exploring everything open to him and enabling him to educate himself.

Elgar's later friend and biographer W. H. Reed writes that his mother 'retained what she read, so that in after years she was able to quote passages from books upon a variety of subjects for the edification of her children.'[11] Reed goes on to claim that Elgar inherited her retentive memory, and this accords with what Wulstan Atkins, a civil engineer, relates about his exceptional ability with crossword puzzles, evidenced by his knowledge of the word 'caisson' (a large watertight chamber, open at the bottom, from which the water is kept out by air pressure and in which construction work may be carried out under water):

I was puzzled, however, as to how Elgar could possibly know so technical and unusual a word. He explained to me that he had come across the word some months earlier and had at once looked it up in a dictionary, as he always did on such occasions, and with his uncanny memory it was there for all time.[12]

We are in no doubt that Ann was much closer to Jerrold Northrop Moore's assessment than De-la-Noy's, even though the latter does have the grace to refer to the sympathetic aspect of her character. Being 'sensitive to the aims and potential of others' is in fact one of the highest marks of character; most people are just full of themselves and see others only very much from their own perspective. We consider that De-la-Noy was wrong in seeing her as without ambition. Quite the reverse: Ann was acutely interested in everything and took delight in all life had to offer. Her enormous desire for self-improvement she shared with many Victorians. (*Self-Help* by the Scottish author and reformer Samuel Smiles sold 20,000 copies within a year of its publication in 1859.)

Moore considers that Ann did nevertheless find life quite a challenge. She did not have an easy life, which is why she deliberately pursued other activities. As he notes in his chapter entitled 'Divisions':

Ann Elgar faced the difficulties of this household as well as she could. And when she could not face them, books and her imagination offered an escape which she never disguised from her children. Lucy recalled: 'I used sometimes to wonder if she had come to the end of her illusions, and she said: "No, and I hope they will last as long as I do; they give colour and variety to life and keep one's heart young."'[13]

She probably had to work on herself a lot and found strength in high-minded wise words. Longfellow, therefore, was very much on her wavelength as he was, of course, for many Victorians. This quotation from Longfellow comes almost at the beginning of her first scrapbook and is dated 'Sept 24 1876':

Beware of dreams! Beware of the illusions of fancy!
Beware of the solemn deceivings of thy vast desires!

Many biographers have stressed her romantic, chivalric feelings as dominating her thought, but clearly she saw beyond these, as did Longfellow, who today is frequently misunderstood in such a light.

We think Ann's occasional references in the scrapbooks to her own difficulties and problems are particularly interesting. It is rare to have a glimpse into someone's most private thoughts about themselves.

We think therefore that she did have to struggle against circumstances in many ways. Moore notes that her keeping busy and her abundant use of imagination undoubtedly helped to keep her going. There was something else too: her profound belief in God.

Ann's religious & spiritual insight
De-la-Noy could interpret her faith as being no more than an emotional prop for the weak, who feel secure when doing what they are told by ecclesiastical authority. This fits in with what is now a conventionally sceptical view of religion. We think it, however, very far from the truth about Ann, who saw her religion in a quite different light. She became a Roman Catholic in 1852, five years before Edward was born. The Jesuit foundation of St George's, according to Moore, 'offered an intellectual engagement to faith not easily available to a young woman of the lower middle class.'[14] She accepted all the outward practices, remaining a church-goer for the rest of her life.

Her understanding of her faith was, however, far deeper than conventional religiosity. She was able to discern between the words proclaimed by the church and reality of what is proclaimed, as is evident from the following contribution to the 'Casket of Jewels' in 'Worcester Papers':

The more we ponder on the excellent doctrine of our Redeemer, the more sublime and impressive it appears to us; but the more we listen to the harangues of the Church ministry, who (sic) attempt the setting forth of that doctrine, the more confused and mystified it seems.

7. Ann's Influence on Edward

She saw her belief in God in spiritual terms, relating to the whole of life. There was no neat compartmentalism for her – no indication in the scrapbooks of a narrow-minded attitude to religion. This links up well with what Lucy wrote in her 'Reflections' of 1912:

> *She always held the absolute belief that all which happens to a good person happens for the best, and whatever is given has proved to be the very thing which is needed, the thing worth having, if we put our small helpless hands into the hands of Compassion, the guiding guarding Hands we shall be lifted up and strengthened for all we have to do.*

This is not the language of a mindless convert but of someone wrestling with real questions, such as how on earth anyone can believe in a God of love when terrible things happen. Lucy went on to give an example:

> *When Father once had a deep and serious illness she drew us together and said: 'Now children, this has to be faced. Be brave and pray always: if he goes, God will help us, and if he is spared to us, 'Blessed be God'.*

The impact that his Catholic upbringing had on Edward can be seen as profound, provided that the all-important distinction between spirituality and religiosity is borne in mind. The increasingly anti-religious atmosphere amongst intellectuals in the late-nineteenth century and twentieth century undoubtedly had an effect on him, but his awareness of a spiritual dimension remained undimmed.

An interesting newspaper comment in 1908 about Elgar's First Symphony compared it with *Ein Heldenleben* of Richard Strauss:

> *In both we see a personality struggling against opposing elements; in both the central figure arouses sympathy by the union of indomitable purpose with purely human despondencies. But here the likeness ends. The Symphony is more spiritual than the tone-poem. We seem to see the conflicts and final higher development from within in Elgar's work, 'from without in the other ... Both seem to speak of love; but in Heldenleben it is a human love, in the Symphony it suggests the amor intellectualis Dei ...*[15]

It is fascinating that Strauss really remained as a kind of successor to Wagner, whilst Elgar, though deeply immersed in Wagner's music, retained his own approach to music.

The impression which Ann's spirituality made on Edward stayed with him all his life, despite the very many negative experiences of religion which made him almost certainly a religious doubter.

An ideal mother

If a child is to make the most of innate talent, it is probably fair to say that all the following aspects of nurture are needed.

1. The sense of being loved, for without that a person lacks the fundamental security of mattering as a human being. Lack of that will dog a person's life throughout.
2. A stimulating environment to explore and be excited by. Children brought up in heavily deprived situations and without proper contact with other people just survive and are otherwise bored.
3. The freedom to explore and experience often the thrill of discovery. A child over-monitored and protected by adults becomes dependent on them instead of learning for him/herself.
4. Adult trust in a child's capabilities acts as a huge stimulus by giving the child sufficient self-confidence to think for him/herself.
5. Conversation with adults who bother to listen to the child and to share interests.
6. An orderly atmosphere in which proper self-discipline is learnt by example, without which little can ever be achieved.
7. A sense of purpose based on values and beliefs which are practised in the home.

We think that Ann as a mother could satisfy all these requirements.

Let us consider, for example, how love of reading is most easily imparted. Here is how a very recent book on education expresses the importance of Ann gathering her family around her at Broadheath, with little Edward on her lap, and reading to them:

> *The young child's first foray into the world of books often begins on the lap of a loved one, where they feel safe and ready to explore. Nestled in a cosy spot, shared book reading becomes a time of bonding and language exposure. The voice of a familiar loved one reading, pausing, explaining words and events, even slightly editing the texts so that the story resonates more strongly with that child creates an ideal space for learning and participation in the reading experience.*[16]

7. Ann's Influence on Edward

Our concluding thoughts about Ann

Ann was a mother who gave Edward love and security and understanding – the best possible start in life. Her wide-ranging interests were so important. The more we have researched her life, the more convinced we have become of the crucial role she played in nurturing Edward's genius.

There are so many facets to her character which profoundly influenced Edward:

- Her deep love of the countryside and of nature in all its seasons.
- Her love of reading and fascination with literature. Ann's instilling her love of reading in Edward was what had been done for Thomas Hardy by his mother, Jemima, a contemporary of Ann and also from a poor background. (See Box E for the remarkable similarities between the upbringing of Elgar and Hardy.)
- Her enquiring mind and tremendous interest in everything.
- Her sense of fun and taking nothing more seriously than is needed.
- Her high moral code and chivalric idealism – she believed in goodness and nobility of character and being the best one can be.
- Her independence of mind and capacity to educate herself.
- Her realistic assessment of life, combined with a lively imagination.
- Her refusal to give way to difficulties and determination to find a way through them.
- Her strong but not narrow religious faith.

Undoubtedly Ann was a remarkable and encouraging role model for Edward. She did not teach him as such but, by example, encouraged that confidence and enthusiasm for learning which was so distinctive of him. It enabled him to turn what otherwise might have been seen as a positive disadvantage in the lack of high-level music education to the creation of his own very individual style.

Edward was, like all deeply perceptive people, prone to potentially debilitating mood swings, close often to depression, hypochondriac and bearing chips on his shoulder. His was not an easy life, yet through it all he retained a sanity, wide-ranging interest in everything, good humour and commitment to the highest in music which never left him. We feel that much of this was due to the example of Ann.

In 1905, when receiving the 'Freedom of the City of Worcester', Elgar confessed that his position was owing to the influence of his mother and many of the things she said to him he had tried to carry out in his music.[17] This was a remarkable acknowledgement by Edward of how much he valued his mother. It was a public occasion and three years after her death. If ever we needed proof of his indebtedness to her, it is in those few words.

In the closing lines of her novel *Middlemarch*, Ann's contemporary George Eliot writes the following lines about her great heroine, Dorothea, that we think could apply to Ann Greening in the context of the part she unwittingly played in her son's great music:

> … *the effect of her being on those around her was incalculably diffusive: for the growing good of the world is partly dependent on unhistoric acts; and that things are not so ill with you and me as they might have been, is half owing to the number who lived faithfully a hidden life, and rest in unvisited tombs.*

7. Ann's Influence on Edward

Box E: Similarities between the Upbringing of Elgar and Hardy

People have remarked on similarities between Elgar's life and that of Thomas Hardy. Both were born (on 2 June) in country cottages in the middle of the nineteenth century and had violin-playing fathers who were somewhat dreamy and mothers of strong character who greatly influenced them. Hardy's mother, Jemima, had been a maidservant and cook from an impoverished background, who acquired a love of reading and developed literary tastes and fostered a love of literature in her son and was greatly ambitious for him – just like Ann with Edward. Unsurprisingly, Elgar and Hardy retained great affection for their mothers, and Hardy wrote a poem to mark Jemima's death, *After the Last Breath*. (Elgar was briefly in contact with Hardy in 1913 through a mutual friend, and the possibility of Elgar basing an opera on a Hardy novel arose – *The Trumpet Major*, *The Return of the Native* and *The Dynasts* were mooted – but Hardy's death in 1928 brought their possible collaboration to an abrupt close.)

Part II

Source Material

8.
Lucy's 'Reflections'

Lucy's family memories, contained in an unpublished document called 'Reflections', shed important light on her mother. We have already quoted them, and Elgar biographers have understandably drawn on them widely.

Lucy had married Charlie Pipe, and Edward spent six years of his bachelorhood with her and her husband. Charlie was a keen observer of the arts and social scene in Worcester, and his memoirs were published in *Berrow's Worcester Journal* in 1972, but it is Lucy's 'Reflections' which throws important light on her mother.

Lucy wrote down her memories of her mother and childhood in June 1912, and they were read and endorsed by 17 people, 10 of whom had known Ann personally. We do not know why she chose to write these 'Reflections' in this semi-public manner. Presumably she had been asked many times to share remembrances of Ann. The timing was also 10 years after Ann had died, so perhaps there was some memorial gathering over which she presided. Copies were certainly sent around and comments dated between August 1912 and October 1913, those from America between November and December 1912.

Not surprisingly the first comment on her memoir was by Charlie, appropriately humorous: 'A cleverly written little sketch of the best mother-in-law I ever had, – and (I) endorse all her daughter has said of her, never shall I forget her smile! And the ringing laughter when I told her a good joke, which she always appreciated and enjoyed.'

A second, most important comment was from Hubert Leicester, who as a child had known Ann so well and been trusted by her with watching over Edward, two years younger than himself. He summed up Ann as simply 'to my mind an ideal woman'. To his wife, Agnes, she 'seemed a saintly woman'.

Other long-standing friends concurred entirely with what Lucy had written – Isabel and Jessie Colney, Elizabeth Garould, Charles Smille, Ida Baylis and Maria Birch. Her nephew and nieces Charles, Clara and Amelia in America also endorsed Lucy's 'Reflections', each mentioning the extensive correspondence which their Aunt Elgar had exchanged with them.

We wonder if Lucy's brothers and sisters were asked for their opinion of her memories. It would seem strange if they were not. Edward for one, though living in London in 1912, was keenly interested in the family history.

Lucy's style of writing is rather a jumble and often does not flow readily. It is not studied prose but more like someone talking and recalling in conversation, further suggesting an informal origin.

The 'Reflections' are a remarkable and precious historical source. They are the closest we can get to a kind of conversation with Ann. Time and again in them Lucy shares Ann's thoughts and comments.

On the purpose of life, Ann would say 'be always busy, doing something that is useful and interesting.' Lucy notes that Ann 'wishes us to be of the crew of this great ship we call the world, and not of its useless passengers.'

Lucy asked her one day whether she would ever come to the end of her illusions, and she said she hoped they would never end, for they enhanced her life.

When walking with Ann in the countryside, she would sometimes say, 'When surrounding nature is so glorious, conversation seems out of place and harmony – the mind becomes filled with thoughts and impressions that cannot be clothed in language.'

The breadth of Ann's religious understanding is shown in this comment that Lucy records: 'God is not far off; we are in God. His ear is close to our life. It is never taken away, even when we dream and sleep, we sigh into it.'

As she grew weaker, she talked with Lucy about death: 'I often wonder what it will be like.' And then she would quote Ruskin: 'Every noble life leaves the fibre of it interwoven with the work of the world.'

We know in any case that her life was far from easy, bringing up seven children with only modest financial means. Moreover, she had the anguish of losing Harry and Joe. Her husband cannot have been an easy person to get on with. He disapproved strongly, for example, of her Catholicism, but she never let that get her down. (Despite his antagonism William had become a Roman Catholic when he died. Perhaps it was a wish to be buried with his wife and deceased children; perhaps also it was the influence of Dot, who had become a nun.) However, Ann and William's relationship appears to have been a loving one.

A common first reaction for the modern reader is to see Lucy as a fantasist, sentimental in her vastly unrealistic portrayal of Ann, depicting her as the ideal mother, who, of course, has never existed. Much of it is written in the luxurious, over-the-top, longwinded prose of the Victorian era and beyond. Thus it begins referring to her notes as:

> ... very slight, but such as they are, they indicate something of the life of my Mother, one of the most charming women on earth, she was truly one of nature's gentlewomen – for, if any woman ever loved beauty and reverently turned to the very soul of Nature, it was my Mother.

8. Lucy's 'Reflections'

She described their life at Broadheath as:

> ... made up by the constant friendship between Mother and children, our life was blessed in an exceptional degree with intellectual sympathy and most thoughtful love.
>
> We were brought up in the very atmosphere of happiness and simple enjoyment of life ... Mother's grace and manners, her whole appearance indeed indicated a mood of serene pleasure – that delightful air of cheerful happiness which surrounds those who can enjoy ordinary life without the excitement of passion or appetite.
>
> There was always that air of comfort and elegance about our home which certain women have the power to impart to their dwelling places.

It is interesting that Lucy notes she did not remember much about their first few years of town life:

> I do not think we were much impressed by other girls' experiences, for we saw in the homes of many of our school friends there was no actual discomfort but no real enjoyment – in our home all was enjoyment and happiness, thanks again to the tact and sweetness of our dear Mother.
>
> She was the true friend, never demanding obligation in any way – What good she did others was always done in the true spirit of friendship so that each one of us in our little troubles, or the thought of coming strife flew to her as a bird flies to its nest at the sudden breaking of the storm, and she shared the perfect confidence of her many friends who always felt they could fully trust her, and know that trust was sacred.
>
> Dear Mother! Hers was such a sensitive mind and vivid imagination, a delicately balanced organisation that almost lived on its ideas as veritable food – She was not only a good wife, she was a pious, beautiful, patient woman – then her smile! It was such a delightful smile, so full of love and pleasure.

Nevertheless, even the most hardened sceptic has to accept that there is a wealth of down-to-earth detail included which makes it an invaluable historical source. A passage like this may seem unrealistically flattering: 'I watched most attentively all the grand and noble character of my dear Mother and the wonderful charm and influence which she had over everybody she came into contact with.' Yet it is followed immediately by reference to Ann's delight in Spring: 'She sought natural joy in her daily pinpricks by taking long walks and commune with Nature ...'

Lucy is, however, also realistic. She speaks, for example, of the 'most important crisis of my life – my marriage – when I took upon myself the hardest task on earth.' (This task might have been persuading Charlie Pipe to convert to Roman Catholicism, which he did but he eventually lapsed, according to his memoirs.) Moreover, Lucy was highly critical of much modern development around her:

> *One half of the population move about as if they had perpetual neuralgia.*
> *I cannot help remembering the change in everything – now we see the simple life, such as we were brought up to, is not the accepted life of the present day – high-born women gamble like stable boys, and well-bred men watch, without a word of monstrance (remonstration?), the open flirtations of their wives ... Then the extravagance of the present youth makes you feel pained and sorry.*

Lucy was dismayed at the state of the cottage at Broadheath:

> *It grieves me to think that the once pretty and charming* Newbury Cottage *(an alternative name for* The Firs*) has become a tumbled-down neglected place ... Our once pretty garden is a complete wilderness, no trace of the fountain, and the lawn has been used for many years as a potato patch! The owner is considered much to blame for allowing so pretty a house to fall into decay for the sake of a little sum of money being spent on necessary repairs at the early stage of its downfall ... Too many of the picturesque half-timbered cottages around the Common then standing have been swept away and replaced by the 'Modern Villa' (a hideous invention).*

We find sentences like this particularly convincing: '(Ann) was a born artist in daily life, and she used daily life as if every moment was to be enjoyed, and to be made use of – she always maintained "The laws of the body, its health and happiness, are as much God's laws as any other."'

> *Her very soul was wrapped up in her husband and her children – she often drove out with Father in the country on his little tours of business, and during the time he was occupied she would sketch the churches and little bits of pleasant scenery, and ... among the flowers. Some of her simple pencillings are very sweet, but she never learnt the art of drawing, so it shows her talent and ability to do almost anything.*

8. Lucy's 'Reflections'

There are four sketches by Ann at the Elgar Birthplace Museum, modest efforts, but most people would be impressed by them. They are evidence of Ann's sensitivity and artistry that were well above average. One sketch is identified as 'Westbury on Severn' and shows the church with detached tower where Ann's parents were married. Another is marked 'Arlingham' (just across the river from Westbury) and dated 22 May 1882 in a strong hand; it is the parish church of St Mary (see Illust. 40). One sketch seems to be marked *Sunrise* and dated '25 June (18)82'. The last one is a view along the river, quite possibly the Severn, and the marking seems to say '(18)82' with a place-name or month that is illegible.

How did these sketches come to be drawn? At least two suggest an excursion to the area south of Gloucester where the Greenings came from. Was Ann accompanying William on a piano-tuning journey? Did she travel alone? Arlingham lies on the eastern bank of the Severn at the end of the 'Horseshoe Bend', where the river flows nine miles to progress one. How did Ann get to this remote place? Did she stay with relatives? We do not know. By 1882 Edward was lodging with his married sister Pollie, and his diary does not refer to his mother making such an excursion. It is significant that the family saw fit to retain the sketches.

We can well imagine that Ann's presence was formidable and could have had an over-dominating effect on her children (note the already-quoted observation of Lucy that she could be severe). Lucy gives an example from when she was much older. She was corrected for criticising the colour of her cousin's necktie when they were visiting Symond's Yat on the Herefordshire/Gloucestershire border, Ann 'almost overcome by the grandeur of the scenery': 'Oh! My blessed Mother! Her face was a picture of indignation at such an outrage – she gasped, "How can you have such a thought when there is so much to inspire one." To me it was a lesson to leave alone people's neckties in future – and I felt very crushed.'

Perhaps it was just as well that Lucy married someone who didn't take life too seriously and had so ready a sense of humour which he could share with Ann.

Conclusions

Lucy's 'Reflections' are important in showing what a powerful impression Ann made on her eldest daughter (and probably all her children). Clearly Ann's appreciation of Edward's specifically impressive talent did not diminish in any way her loving regard for her other children.

She was romantic by temperament, and poetic by nature; she had the unmistakable air of good breeding which, like the perfect manners of the true gentlewoman, is felt without being defined – being highly educated, with fine

40. Sketch by Ann of St Mary's Church, Arlingham, near Gloucester, dated 22 May 1882.

8. Lucy's 'Reflections'

literary tastes and a deep reader all her life, and what is more to the point, in her conversation there was always something well worth remembering.

She might have shone in many other walks of life, but in none could she have left such a happy memorial behind as will remain in the hearts and homes of those who have had the estimable benefit of her guidance during those impressionable years when character is formed, and ideals of life are implanted.

We think that Lucy was right in what she says here. The strong, but basically good, character of Ann did provide the young Edward with the nurture his genius needed. It may indeed be the case that Ann herself had the incredible retentive memory which Edward had. This would account for the breadth and depth of Ann's interest in life which spilled over into the lives of all her children.

9.
Ann's Scrapbooks

Ann began the first of two scrapbooks on 24 September 1876 at the age of 54. Her five surviving children were still at home but making fewer demands on her, the youngest, Dot, then aged 12. We still wonder how she found the time to do it at all, looking after the house and family. The second scrapbook was started in 1889 when she was 67 and completed probably in July 1893 when she was 71, as that is the last date in her writing. See Illust. 41-44 for examples.

To open Ann's scrapbooks is to realise at once that she was a woman of enormous interests and an inquisitive mind. Was she searching for the education she sadly lacked as a child? The scrapbooks give us a clue in this direction in that so often the arrangement of the material is haphazard. An article catches her attention, but she does not relate it to any particular theme. In order to get as much of interest onto the page, items were arranged regardless of subject matter. Just occasionally she recorded precise dates. We get the feeling that she was merely enjoying herself: keeping a scrapbook was, of course, a popular hobby in Victorian times.

We can imagine Ann cutting out everything of interest, but she also wanted to create something she found pleasing to her eye. She was certainly determined not to waste any space, so every inch was filled.

Her handwriting is that of a strong and determined character, mostly easy to read but not entirely legible. Some extracts from journals and other sources appear in very small print: she must have had remarkably good eyesight.

Here is a typical page as an example of what attracted her attention – a complete jumble – but her eyes were open to everything. By a picture of the Colonnade Temperance & Commercial Hotel, New Street, Birmingham, she notes, 'Nellie Weaver and I slept here on the night of Dec 13th, 1883, after a performance of (Edward's) *Intermezzo Moresque*. We went on to Coventry next day.' On the same page she has an announcement of the death of 'Mr Henry Perkes in London, formally (sic) of this city'. Alongside, was a print of a castle, a Norman arch from Canterbury, a windmill, a seascape, an historical cartoon of Dürer, showing a first design for the triumphal carriage (1514-1515) of the Emperor Maximilian I, and a cutting of a poem:

9. Ann's Scrapbooks

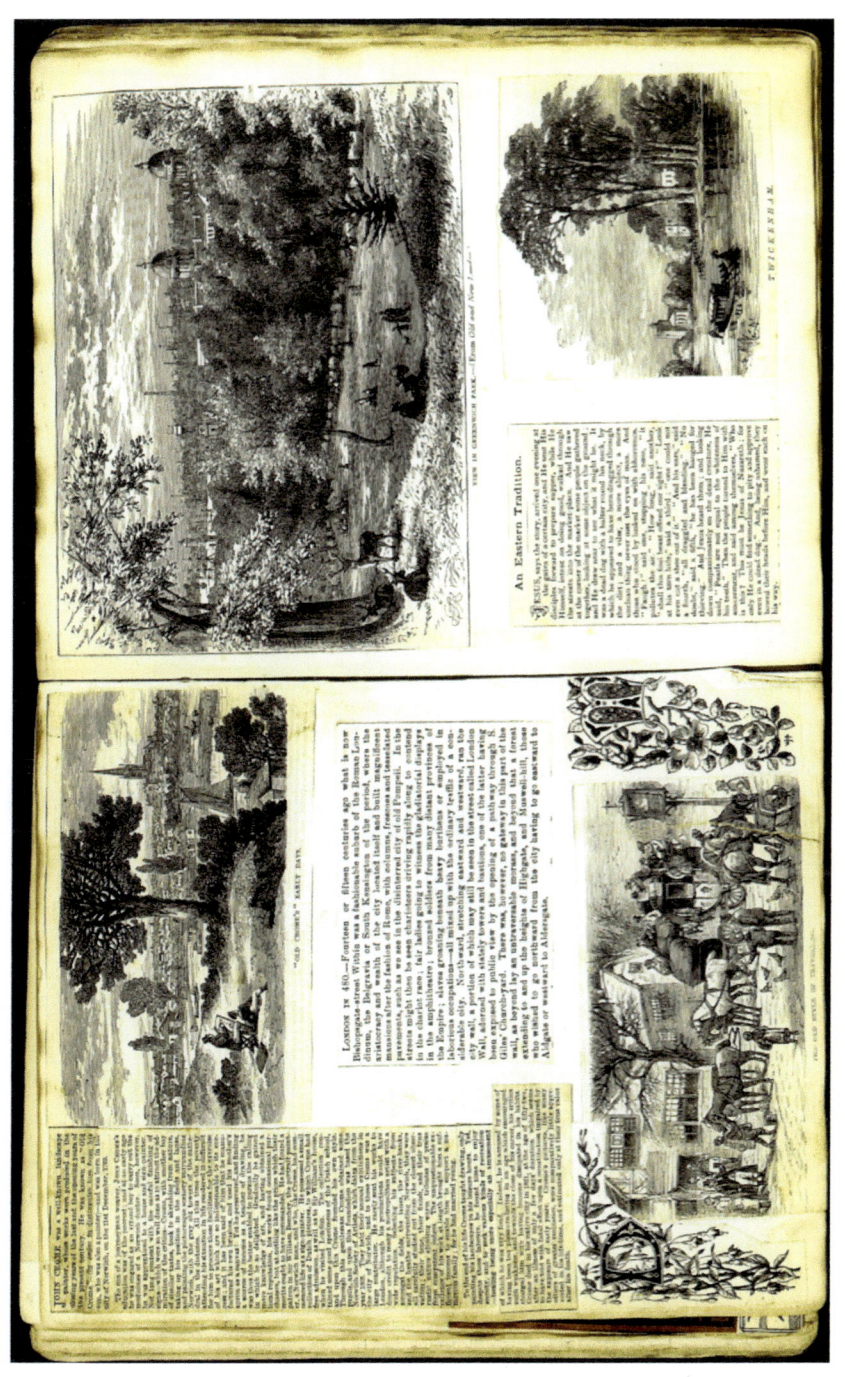

41. A page from Ann's scrapbook.

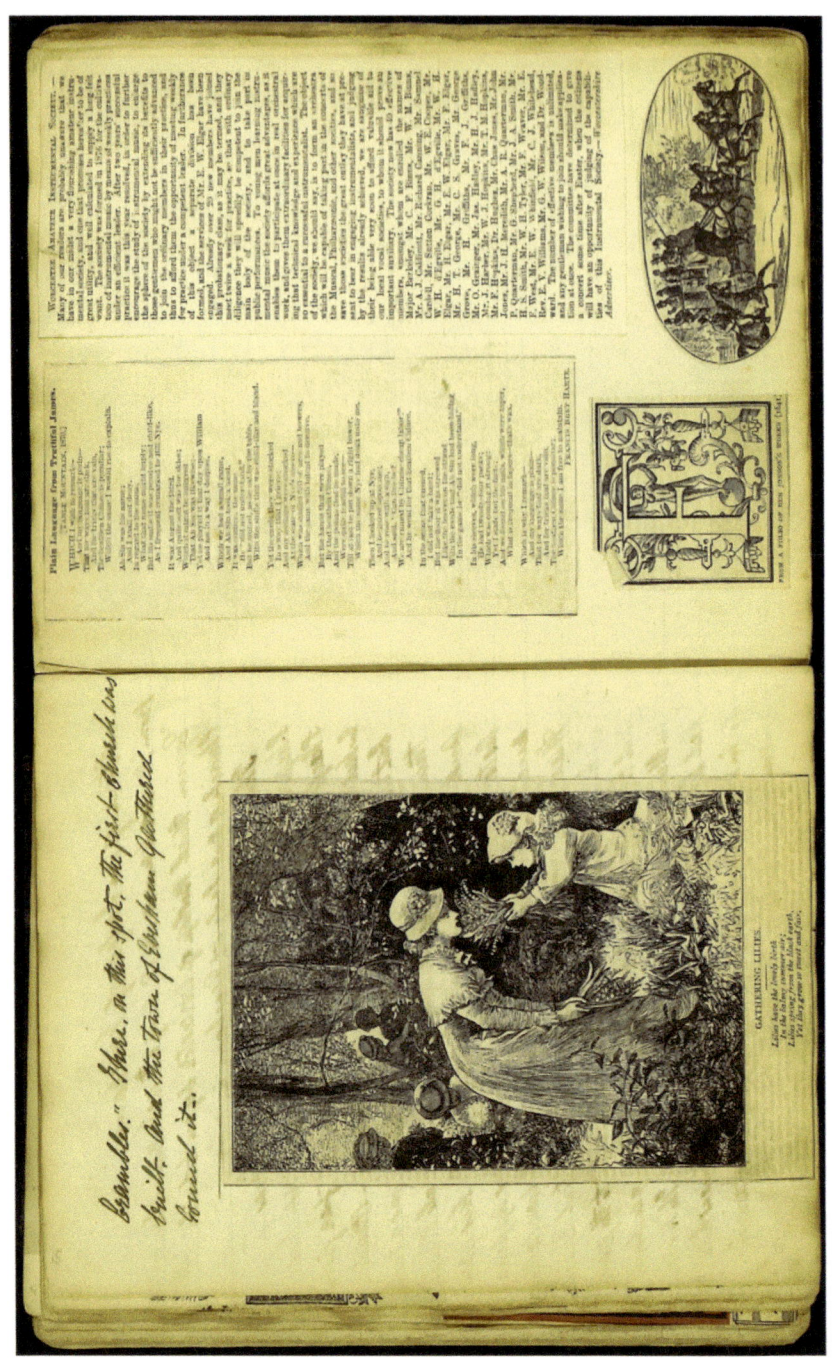

42. A page from Ann's scrapbook.

9. Ann's Scrapbooks

43. A page from Ann's scrapbook.

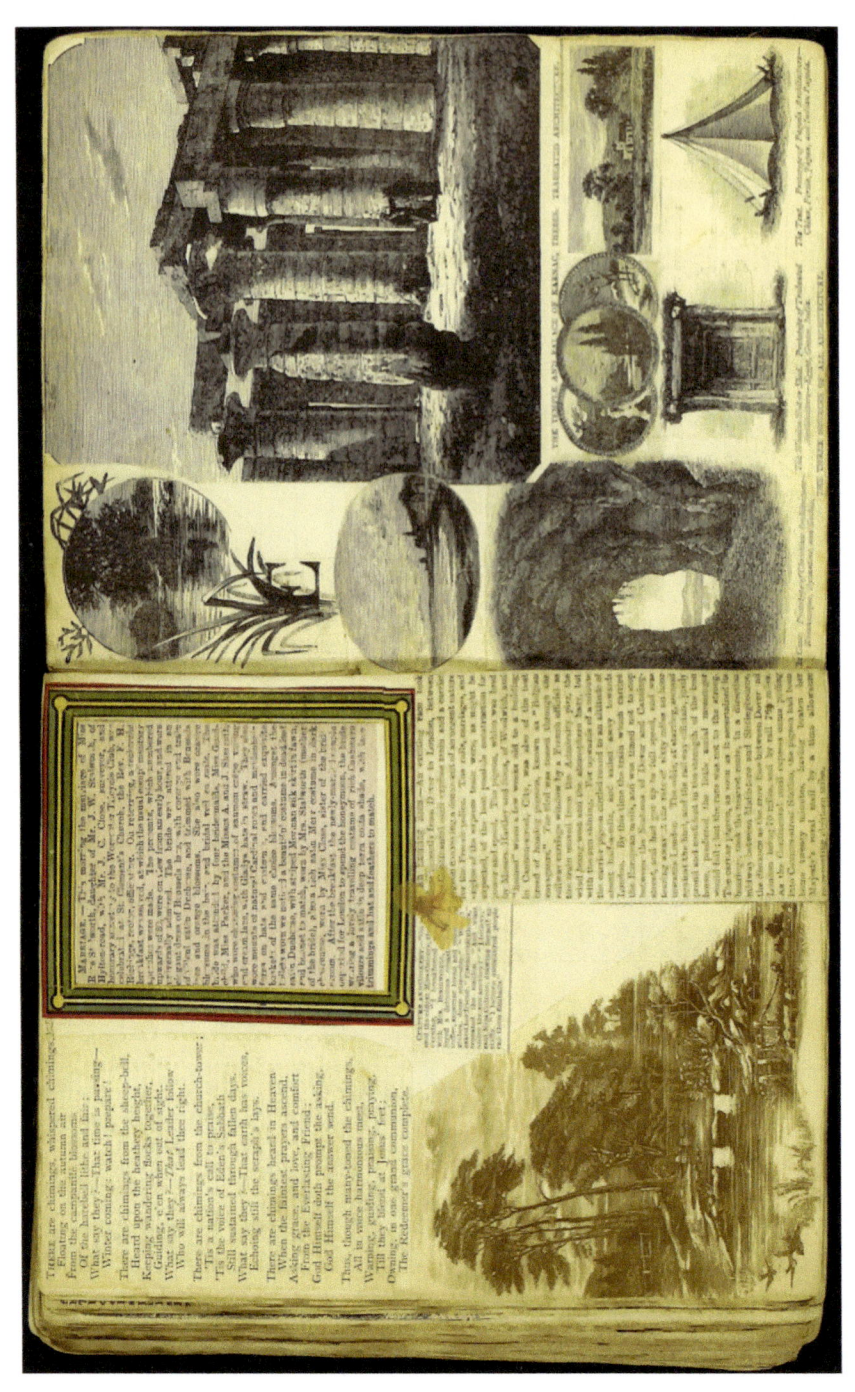

44. A page from Ann's scrapbook.

9. Ann's Scrapbooks

Suppose you've got a holiday,
And the rain comes pouring down,
Will it clear off any sooner
Because you scold and frown?
And wouldn't it be better
For you to smile than pout,
And so make sunshine in the house
When there's none without?

The scrapbooks show how wide her interests were. Fascination with the world is something she undoubtedly passed on to Edward; he responded by converting this into music of the highest quality.

There were certain themes which clearly commanded her attention, such as architecture, with, for example, pictures of Peterborough Cathedral and Clifton Suspension Bridge, and a long extract on the restoration of St Osburg's Church, Coventry. We assume that the pictures of the Belfry at Bruges and of Cologne Cathedral reminded her of Edward's holidays abroad – he had sent her several postcards.

History was important to her, and there are snippets of archaeological significance. For example, she gives a very long quotation in her own meticulous handwriting of a major discovery of royal remains in ancient Egypt.

Local events are noted, e.g., a picture of the new Railway Hotel in Malvern (the Imperial Hotel of 1862, which became Malvern Girls' College in 1919). There is a fascinating comment about Thomas Carlyle's hostile attitude to the hydrotherapy he experienced in Malvern, written by Miss Gully, whose father was the distinguished doctor responsible for the water cure. Still very locally, there is a very full and interesting description of the break-up of the frost, causing flooding of the Severn in 1883. All kinds of other unconnected subjects appear, such as stories as 'Our Lady of Evesham', reference to the Knights Templar from a Worcestershire book on chivalry, a strong argument for Penny Postage, information about printing, reference to the medieval allegorical poem *Piers Plowman*, a piece on various uses of ammonia, the obituary of a Worcester Catholic surgeon, William Allen, etc.

She also notes a meeting called by Sir Peter Allsopp at *Battenhall Mount* in Worcester to discuss the formation of a new orchestral society for Worcester and County, although there were no Elgars involved – we can assume that Edward was now in London and Frank was probably busy with his wind band.

She pasted in a printed poem by Alice, published under her maiden name, entitled *Question and Answer*.

The arts and artists get some mention, and there are a number of literary references, including Longfellow, Wordsworth, Coleridge, Thomas Campbell, Walter Scott, Walt Whitman, Oscar Wilde and Rudyard Kipling.

Poetry clearly meant a great deal to Ann. Throughout her life she would write poems, and the scrapbooks have examples. Her dog Tip died on 15 July 1885 and she writes:

My Faithful Tip
What shall I write for today?
Why do we records keep?
When they only have to say
Something to make us weep.

'My Treasures' refers to cards received from various people in an album, a reference possibly to her 'sailor brother'. We think she wrote it because usually she is careful to put in inverted commas to show that something is copied, and here she has not.

My Treasures
They are kept in a little volume
That has edges all worn and frayed,
That has pages I smile to look on,
That has bits that my tears had made.

There're cards sent by childish painters
Who were tutor'd by love, not art.
These are better whose rhymes are faulty
Yet I know every word by heart.

There's a card from a sailor brother,
Just an anchor with hearts above;
Here's another, all gold and crimson
For dear mother with baby's love.

Little cards, I can find a record
Of the story of days gone by
As I tenderly turn the pages
Of the volume wherein you lie.

May 29 1881

9. Ann's Scrapbooks

There is a possibility that one should be included under the poems she wrote:

I heard a brooklet gushing
From its rocky fountain near
And down the valley
So fresh and wondrous clear.

Here is an interesting piece on Lord Tennyson's new poems:

They are slaves who fail to speak for the fallen and the weak.

A poem by the American Romantic poet James Russell Lowell may be relevant for our times.

There is a long poem, *The Painter of Seville,* in which Murillo gives his slave freedom, knowing he will be a greater painter than himself.

On the last page in the scrapbook is this poem on the importance of hope and optimism:

The rain is on the river,
But the sun is on the hill …
'Tis the winter's white snow-shower
That defends the shiv'ring root
'Tis the falling of the flower that gives birth unto the fruit.
Then arise from helpless moping,
Nor repine at each annoy.
There is room for wider hoping
If your days are void of joy …

This poem is relevant to us today as then. It sums up her character well as always trying to look on the bright side of things, rather than wallowing in what is depressing.

There are many aphorisms and wise thoughts scattered through the scrapbooks, for example:

When we can only think and cannot dream, then we are truly old.
As in a man's life, so in his studies, it is the most beautiful and human thing in the world so to mingle gravity with pleasure that the one may not sink into melancholy nor the other rise into wantonness.

Most men have hobbies, this one books, that one fame, the other pelf.*
But heaven protect us from the man whose hobby is himself.
(*Pelf is money, probably dishonestly gained.)

Geoffrey Trease, the prolific writer, memorably described Ann as 'a country-woman from the Forest of Dean, who loved Nature and preferred poetry to pots and pans.'[1] Trease lived for many years at Colwall and was probably aware that Ann was staying here when she urged Edward to write music about the hill fort known as The British Camp.

Ann definitely had a sense of humour and was alive to it in others. Here are some examples:

- An advert letting out teeth for the evening! This comes shortly after her own sad comment about losing her last tooth.
- A cartoon of a bull chasing a painter over a stile.

A lot of her humour involved animals or birds, e.g., a rationalist chicken; a cockerel riding a penny-farthing; a humorous sonnet about a languishing linnet.

Some of it showed quick wit, e.g., 'A gentleman at an eating-house asked the person next to him if he would please pass the mustard. "Sir, do you mistake me for the waiter?" "No, sir, I mistook you for a gentleman."'

Ann found amusing an advert for Pears soap, using a line from *The Jackdaw of Rheims* by Richard Harris Barham: 'Worthy of washing the hands of the Pope.'

What bad temper costs: 'Talking of "losing the temper" reminds me of the old gentleman who said he wished he could lose his temper "for I confess", he continued, "that it is a very bad one."'

On the last page of the second scrapbook is a drawing of 'A work of Heart'. Is that a fitting way to describe the scrapbooks as a whole?

Religion per se is not mentioned much in the scrapbooks, but it clearly underlies her attitude to life in general. She noted that Fr Waterworth left Worcester in November 1878 after 20 years of residence and that he came back to visit her. He was probably a strong influence on her. What is interesting, however, is that his strongly dogmatic attitude towards Roman Catholicism does not seem to have affected her. There is no indication in the scrapbooks of a narrow-minded attitude to religion. She includes a simple prayer, for example, which links up well with what Lucy wrote about her trust in God, but there is nothing specifically Catholic about it; it could be said by any Christian, and indeed by any devout Muslim or Hindu:

9. Ann's Scrapbooks

I do not ask my path to understand
My way to see
Better in darkness just to feel Thy hand
And follow Thee.

She quotes a letter on the question, Was Shakespeare a Catholic? It reflects a very moderate view, with which most scholars today would agree:

If the evidence that can be produced on the subject is, after all, inconclusive, it is nevertheless certain that the scale and spirit of his writings are uniformly respectful towards the virtues and office of the Catholic Church.

Perhaps Ann was like Nana in Chekhov's play *Uncle Vanya*: wise with a strong faith in God that illuminated all she did and helped her to cope with all the difficulties and distresses that turned up, with the boredom of duties, with the intelligent sensitivity of a countrywoman at home with nature.

10.

'Worcester Papers'

In spite of her husband's intolerance of Roman Catholicism, Ann and William had much in common, as their lively interest in local and national affairs shows. They compiled what they termed 'Worcester Papers' in extensive correspondence with the Elgars in Kent, who called their contribution 'The Dover News'. Ann contributed independently from her husband, denoting her entries with **, whilst William's were marked +++. Some of Ann's contributions are presented in the Appendix, essays addressing such weighty issues as capital punishment and sanitation. The prose is the longwinded style beloved of Victorians, but the writings clearly show a provincial housewife of rudimentary education engaging with current affairs to an extraordinary degree.

'Worcester Papers' No.1 deals with capital punishment. Attitudes towards the punishment of crimes began to change during the nineteenth century: retribution became less important as belief in the reforming of prisoners increased. The century started with the death penalty for pickpockets, but, as the years passed, the number of capital offences dropped from hundreds to just five by 1861: murder, treason, piracy with violence, espionage and the burning down of a weapons store or navy dockyard. Nevertheless, Ann's views in 1852 can now be seen as progressive. Her essay alludes to Mary Robins (1825-1903), a young mother and needlewoman, who was convicted at Worcester Assizes of 'destroying her own child, 14 days old'. Commutation of the sentence of death was granted on the ground that she was of feeble mind. She was transported to Van Diemen's Land (Tasmania) with 218 other convicts on the *Duchess of Northumberland* on 25 November 1852. There is also reference to phrenology, a pseudoscience based on the notion that the shapes of people's heads are a guide to their personalities.

'Worcester Papers' No.4 deals with the inadequate provision for public sanitation in Worcester. It was written by Ann at the age of about 30, four years into her marriage. It essentially makes a powerful case (paraphrased):

No nation can prosper without a healthy population, so it is high time the public authorities provided us with a system of drainage and sewerage. Who would deny their fellow creatures these prerequisites for a healthy life? Yet there are people trying to block the 'Health of Towns' Act in Worcester! Are they doing so because it would cost them a little more?

10. 'Worcester Papers'

Ann quotes Joseph Hume, F.R.S., a doctor and M.P. involved in the national effort to improve public sanitation. Putting aside the prolixity of the writing and the absence of facts on the specific situation in Worcester, her grasp of the subject is remarkable. She suspects that sanitary reform is being resisted by people who are afraid because it will cost them more in taxation:

And we are given to understand, that there are some of this class of people who are now actively exerting themselves to prevent if possible the necessary steps being taken for the carrying out of the object of the "Health of Towns Act" in the city of Worcester, etc.

Ann also recognises that employers need to show respect to their employees as they expect the same from them:

... we must have less distinction between the upper classes and the lower classes – more of that spirit of kindness one towards another which is essential to the happiness and contentment of every degree of station in this life, etc.

Interest in civic developments was clearly passed on to Ann's son Edward, as evidenced by his foreword to the book *Forgotten Worcester* by his childhood friend and neighbour Hubert Leicester (later Mayor of Worcester):

Nothing escaped our notice; everything was discussed and adjudicated upon ... I recall a report in the Journal of a committee in which it was advised that an outlying street should be 'curbed and channelled'.[1]

Some of Ann's words are quoted by Percy Young in his Elgar biography, where he alludes to the parlous state of sanitation in Worcester and a 'vigorous, obstructive, and vociferous "anti-sanitation" party in the city'.[2]

'Worcester Papers' No.5 deals with the great Severn flooding in 1852. The middle years of the nineteenth century were notable for Severn floods: 1845, 1847, 1852, 1862 and 1868. An antique print was made of men in a boat rescuing sheep at Powick Ham in 1852 and reproduced in *The Illustrated London News*. However, the greatest flood is thought to have occurred in May 1886, when the Severn almost submerged the arches of Worcester Bridge and a man caught a pike in the sitting room of the nearby *Old Rectifying House*. Ann put a newspaper cutting in her scrapbook of the Severn freezing over in 1883 (as it did in 1855 and 1879) and being used for skating. During the thaw the river rose by 6 ft in 12 hours, and huge blocks of ice rushed downstream, sweeping away boats and blocking Worcester

Bridge. Edward would observe the 1862, 1868 and 1883 floods, and, on his way to school, would pass through the fourteenth-century Watergate by Worcester Cathedral, where the flood levels are indelibly recorded in stone.

'A Casket of Jewels'
Distributed between the six editions of 'Worcester Papers' at this time are 21 reflections on life under the heading 'A Casket of Jewels'. Seventeen are from Ann, one by William and two by others identified only as M, Amazon and Henrietta. Ann's reflections show her to be thoughtful, philosophical, somewhat cynical, deeply religious and proud of her womanhood. We have quoted some already; here is a selection of the others. The following interesting observation seems to mean more than simply 'judge not by appearances':

> *As the blackest mineral can bestow the greatest comfort, so can the darkest minds inspire delight.*

This observation shows realism:

> *A man without friends is like a ship without a rudder, cast upon the boundless ocean, and insultingly tossed hither and thither by the angry waves.*

The following contributions are strangely cynical, not the philosophy of a romantic:

> *Do not suppose your warmest friends to be your best friends or probably you will be deceived – recollect the sweetest and most tempting fruit generally contains the maggot.*
>
> *There are tears of joy and there are tears of sorrow, each springing from the same well – the one are the first pure pourings of the crystal fount sweetened with gratitude; the others are the dregs which remain at the bottom, impregnated with bitterness and the softenings of humiliation.*

In contrast to Ann's vein of cynicism, here are several positive thoughts of hope:

> *The sweetest fruits have invariably the roughest rind; so have the best-tempered folks the most uncouth appearance.*
>
> *It will scarcely be thought practicable to some, that we are all capable to a measured extent, of doing a great amount of good to the rest of mankind.*
>
> *With a sound heart and a good character no one need ever despair of finding a partner.*

Part III

Background Information

11.
The Place of Women in Victorian Society

Ann lived through a period when the notion of women's rights was seriously beginning to be raised. Queen Victoria called it 'The Woman Question'. The English novelist and writer Mary Wollstonecraft, who found herself in France during the French Revolution and publicly complained that women were excluded from citizen rights (her *Vindications of the Rights of Women* was published in 1792), provided inspiration for many other writers, including Jane Austen, George Eliot and Elizabeth Barrett Browning. The first pamphlets in favour of the enfranchisement of women began to appear in the middle of the nineteenth century. John Stuart Mill presented a petition in Parliament calling for the inclusion of women's suffrage in the Reform Act of 1867. His book, published in 1869 on *The Subjection of Women,* powerfully raised the issues. As the century wore on, there was increasing demand that women should be given equal rights with men politically, legally, in education and economically.

Ann in her scrapbooks shows an interest in how women are viewed but she does not appear to have shown any special interest in the new feminism. This is probably because at that time of her life she had so many other concerns and interests. Therefore, although Ann should not be thought of as an early feminist, her independence of mind and lively interest in many aspects of public life and welfare, as evidenced especially in her contribution to the 'Worcester Papers' as well as in her scrapbooks, suggest that for her the two spheres of influence were not hermetically sealed. In practice the life she lived and the influence she had on others may fairly be said to have played a part in changing the stereotyped perception of women. It was not, of course, until after the cataclysmic experience of World War I, when women, of necessity, took over many jobs deemed only suitable for men, that former negative attitudes towards the capabilities of women died away sufficiently to allow them the vote. But throughout the nineteenth century many women had played much more than a background part and thus prepared the ground for women's emancipation, and among that number was Ann with her sturdy independence of mind and quiet leadership qualities.

12.

Concern for Schooling in the Pre-Victorian Period

Hannah More
Both poet and playwright, Hannah More (1745–1833) became a friend of leading cultural and literary figures in London, including Joshua Reynolds, David Garrick and Dr Johnson. She energetically supported another friend, William Wilberforce, in his campaign for the abolition of slavery, writing a very long, emotionally powerful poem on the evil of slavery to coincide with the parliamentary debate he initiated:

Shall Britain where the soul of freedom reigns,
Forge chains for others she disdains?
Forbid it, Heaven! O let the nations know
The liberty she loves she will bestow.

Here are some bon mots of hers:

Obstacles are those frightful things you see when you take your eyes off the goal.
    Forgiveness is the economy of the heart … forgiveness saves the expenses of anger, the cost of hatred, the waste of spirits.
    How goodness heightens beauty.

She was also famous for the Sunday schools she set up with her sisters. Relative to the schooling activities of her day, Sunday schools associated with the More sisters had a more informal air and used a range of methods. There was more of a concern with creating the right atmosphere and relationship for learning. Besides classes, there were other community and welfare interventions plus some concern with social life.

Hannah More wrote a book called *Hints on How to Run a Sunday School*, in which she wrote that programmes had to be planned and suited to the level of the students. There also needed, she said, to be variety in education, with classes as entertaining as possible, including singing. She was more progressive than many educationists today!

She knew of the work of Robert Raikes (1736-1811), who was a little older than her and operated in Gloucester. He is strongly connected with Sunday schools – he did not invent them but firmly established them through his publishing connections. There was much criticism of the movement. Opponents regarded them as 'desecrating the Sabbath'. They considered that teaching the common people to read risked stirring up a French-style revolution. In fact, in the very year when that revolution started, 1789, Hannah More copied Raikes in setting up her first Sunday school at Wilberforce's suggestion. It is worth noting that the famous economist Adam Smith gave the Sunday school movement his strongest commendation:

> *No plan has promised to effect a change of manners with equal ease and simplicity since the days of the Apostles.*

There is a notable connection with the Elgars, for Raikes's great-granddaughter Alice Roberts was to marry Edward Elgar in 1889. Raikes was born in Gloucester in 1736, within nine years of Hannah More's birth in Bristol.

Education & reading in the early nineteenth century
When Ann was ready for school in about 1827, those who could afford it could send their children to private schools. Educational provision for the rest of society was, however, lamentable. Religious organisations were the first to try to give education to the poor. The National Schools were set up in 1811 by the Anglican National Society for Promoting the Education of the Poor. From 1808 there were British Schools, founded by non-conformist and evangelical Christians such as Joseph Fox, William Allen and Samuel Whitbread. From 1818 there were the Ragged Schools, set up by John Pounds to teach the three Rs to poor children. Most common throughout most of the nineteenth century were 'dame schools', where tuition was by a school 'dame', a local woman who would charge a modest fee. From 1863-1866 Edward Elgar attended Miss Walsh's Dame School in Britannia Square, Worcester.

There was nothing similar in England to the mass-education programme which was happening in Prussia. In 1811, emanating from the newly founded University of Berlin, the intention was to educate the whole of the Prussian people. G. M. Trevelyan in his *English Social History* notes that such an attempt at mass education in Britain did not begin before Gladstone's Education Act bill in 1870. He writes, however, a criticism of the Prussian programme which, in the light of subsequent history, may be considered momentous:

The paternal rulers of Germany in the early nineteenth century educated their subjects but gave little political freedom and no share in government. The English State gave the common people great political freedom and some share in government, but let them be educated by private religious charity.[1]

The later metamorphosis of education into obedience to superiors prepared the ground to strangle Germany with the rise of Nazism.

What happened in England was, by contrast, messy and disorganised, but it did allow for the development of different ideas for education, many of these being sound and avoiding the dangers of uniformity. Religious organisations were able to create schools quite different in their ethos. Reformers like Hannah More experimented with what today may be seen as modern approaches, allowing children greater freedom because of their varying circumstances and dispositions.

Reading certainly became widely recognised as an important way to educate, and this went hand in hand with the development of mass literacy. Ann's love of books and reading was certainly in tune with the times in which she lived.

13.
The American Connection – Nineteenth-century Emigration

In 1847 Ann's brother, John, sailed from Liverpool with his family for a new life in America. His sister, Elizabeth, went to see him off after he had said his goodbyes to his ageing parents and his sister Ann back in Claines.

Ann maintained a correspondence with her brother and his family of seven children in America. John Greening had always wanted to be a farmer: he joined the British Temperance Emigration Society and was chosen by them to take up a farm in Wisconsin. He emigrated with his wife, Maria, and their three young children, James, Clara and Charles, and wrote a detailed account of their punishing journey from Liverpool to New Orleans and then by steamboat up the Mississippi to Wisconsin on the borders of Canada by Lake Superior (see Box F, Extracts from John's 'Journal of a Voyage from Liverpool to New Orleans'). On 11 October, in some excitement, he wrote in his journal: 'I struck the first furrow in my own land.'

And later in November he wrote to his parents and sisters, describing his new surroundings: 'I wish I could send you some of our prairie flowers, they are very beautiful and in such variety and profusion …' We can just imagine Ann's delight in his enthusiasm for nature. How proud too she was of his obvious success out there when he became the senior Justice of the Peace and Chairman of the Supervisors for the township of Mazomanie; he then had no time to continue his journal. See map, Illust. 45.

From being a boot-and-shoe-maker in Worcester, John Greening became a self-sufficient farmer, cultivating over 160 acres, building his own house and becoming the most respected man in his community in America. Michael Greening notes: 'Like his sisters in England, he was largely self-educated. He was a very fine example of the strong, intelligent, human and wise men that the Victorian age produced'.[1] John died on 22 February 1900, aged 84.

John Greening's younger son, Charles (Illust. 46), became quite an important person, a tin-smith and then a banker, who was elected to the State legislature in 1876. He named his eldest son Elgar.

45. Map of Wisconsin, U.S.A., showing John Greening's adopted town of Mazomanie.

13. The American Connection – Nineteenth-century Emigration

46. *Charles Greening, one of Ann's American nephews, who came to Worcester in 1900 to visit Ann.*

Box F: Extracts from John Greening's Journal

A voyage from Liverpool to New Orleans on the sailing ship *Radilis*

Sailed from Liverpool April 2nd 1847 (Good Friday)

April 5. All put on half allowance of water already and all sick for three days past. Tis very windy, we take observations daily at 12 o'clock and find ourselves 400 miles from Liverpool today and abominably crowded.

April 19. The grinding and creaking at night banishes sleep for a while, until at last we sink off and forget all around us. Then it is that home becomes most vivid to the mind. We tell our dreams of home and kind friends we have left forever. But I am growing gloomy and that won't suit my own health or those about me.

April 23. We had a sad robbery last night in the steerage, a poor lad had his box broken open and lost every rag he had. The captain won't do anything or interfere, and we have all found out that he cares no more for the comfort of his passengers than if it was a slave ship ... The ship is his own, and he just complies with the act and that is all.

We have no water closet convenience, it being out of order. Shame, shame.

May 3. Becalmed all day with a vertical sun and no shadow at all. Very hot. 88 between decks, 84 on deck in the shade and 109 in the sun. Not going one mile an hour. This is awful.

May 12. Dr McDonnell caught a swallow on the ship this morning, quite exhausted on its way to Europe. I gave it some water and it drank freely in my hand. I breathed a little prayer for the little voyager, hoping it will twitter sweetly in the land of my birth. I let it go its way that I shall never travel again.

May 23. Whitsunday, seven weeks and two days out. We shall get in a few hours now. Oh that my wanderings were over, tis a long way and near 2000 miles to go yet (up the Mississippi River).

Continuation by Maria

Dear friends, we got to Galena on Sunday June 6, at half past one in the morning and had to take our luggage off by torchlight. With John so ill, he was not able to help at all ... The next day at about 4 o'clock we got to the Cotterells' home. John was so ill he could hardly scarcely get out of the wagon, with cramp in the stomach and a violent cough. We are still at the Cotterells' and I am not well myself. The children are quite well and I hope soon to have better news to send you.

14.
Chronology

1822   Ann is born in the parish of Weston-under-Penyard, Herefordshire, to Joseph and Esther Greening.
1830s   Ann's older sister and brother move to Worcester. Ann joins them later.
c.1840   Ann's parents move to the parish of Claines, Worcester.
1841   William Elgar arrives in Worcester to find work in the music business. He meets Ann at the *Shades Tavern*, at which she helps her sister, Elizabeth.
1842   William Elgar is appointed organist at St George's Roman Catholic Church in Worcester.
1847   Ann's brother, John Greening, emigrates to America.
1848   Ann marries William Elgar in London, they set up home at 2 College Precincts, Worcester, and their first child, Harry, is born. Ann's father, Joseph Greening, dies.
1852   Ann's daughter Lucy is born, and Ann is received into the Roman Catholic Church. Ann and William write their 'Worcester Papers' for William's family in Kent. Ann's mother, Esther, dies.
1854   Ann's daughter Pollie (Susanna) is born.
1856   The Elgars move to *The Firs* at Broadheath outside Worcester.
1857   Ann's son Edward is born at Broadheath.
1859   The Elgars move back into Worcester to 1 Edgar Street (not the current house of that address), and their son Joe is born.
1861   The Elgars return to 2 College Precincts, and their son Frank is born.
1863   The Elgars move to 10 High Street and live above their music shop, Elgar Brothers. Ann's sister, Elizabeth, dies. Edward goes to Miss Walsh's Dame School at 11 Britannia Square, Worcester, with Lucy and Pollie.
1864   Ann's daughter and last child, Dot (Helen), is born, and Harry dies at 15 of kidney disease after contracting scarlet fever.
1866   Joe dies of tuberculosis at seven. Edward goes to a Catholic school run by nuns at *Spetchley Park* outside Worcester.
1867   Edward starts his last school, *Littleton House,* at Lower Wick, Worcester.

1872   Edward leaves school at 15 and works for a year in a solicitor's office before working in the family music shop.
1879   Pollie leaves home and marries Will Grafton, and Edward goes to live with them.
1880   Ann's first grandchild, May Grafton, is born to Pollie.
1881   Lucy leaves home and marries Charlie Pipe.
1883   Edward moves to live with the Pipes when the Graftons move away from Worcester. For some months he is engaged to Helen Weaver. St George's Roman Catholic Church replaces William as organist after 37 years.
1885   St George's Roman Catholic Church appoints Edward as organist.
1888   Edward becomes engaged to (Caroline) Alice Roberts.
1889   Edward marries Alice Roberts in London, and they soon move there. Frank leaves home and marries Agnes Bamford.
1890   Ann's grandchild Carice is born in London to Edward and Alice.
1891   Edward and Alice return to Worcestershire to Malvern.
1896   First performance of Edward's *King Olaf*.
1898   Ann and William's Golden Wedding Anniversary.
1899   First performance of Edward's *Enigma Variations*.
1900   Ann's nephew Charles Greening visits her from America. Ann's brother, John Greening, dies.
1901   Edward's *The Dream of Gerontius* (1900) secures him international recognition after a performance in Germany.
1902   Ann dies in Worcester at 80 and is buried at the city's Astwood Cemetery.
         In the following few years, Edward receives a knighthood (1904) and the 'Freedom of the City of Worcester' (1905), and Ann's husband of 54 years, William Elgar, dies in Worcester in 1906 at 84.

15.
Sources & Bibliography

* especially recommended

Allen, Kevin, *Elgar in Love* (published by author, 2000)
Atkins, E. Wulstan, *The Elgar-Atkins Friendship* (David & Charles, 1984)
Braym, Nina et al (ed.), *The Norton Anthology of American Literature* (W. W. Norton, 2013)
Buckley, R. J., *Sir Edward Elgar* (The Bodley Head, 1905)
Burley, Rosa & Frank C. Carruthers, *Edward Elgar, the Record of a Friendship* (Barrie & Jenkins, 1972)
Cobbett, William, *Rural Rides* (J. M. Dent & Sons, 1912)
De-la-Noy, Michael, *Elgar the Man* (Allen Lane, 1983)
Doolan, Fr Brian, *St George's, Worcester, 1599-1999* (Archdiocese of Birmingham Historical Commission, 1999)
Eickhoff, Dr Louie, *Elgar: What Lay Behind*, article in *Elgar Society Journal*, September 1986
Greening, Michael, *A Family Story: The Greenings & Some of their Relatives* (Matador, 2006)
Gwilliam, H. W., *Old Worcester, People & Places* (Halfshire, 1993)
Kennedy, Michael, *Portrait of Elgar* (Oxford University Press, 1982)*
Leicester, Hubert A., *Notes on Catholic Worcester* (1928) (The National Archives)
Leicester, Hubert A., *Forgotten Worcester* (Ebenezer Bayliss, The Trinity Press, 1930)
Maine, Basil, *Elgar: His Life & Works* (G. Bell & Sons, 1933)
McGuire, Charles Edward, *Measure of a Man: Catechizing Elgar's Catholic Avatars*, article in *Edward Elgar and His World* (Princeton University Press, 2007)
McVeagh, Diana, *Elgar the Music Maker* (Boydell & Brewer, 2007)
Moore, Jerrold Northrop, *Edward Elgar, A Creative Life* (OUP, 1984)*
Moore, Jerrold Northrop, *Spirit of England: Edward Elgar in his World* (Heinemann, 1984)
Moore, Jerrold Northrop (ed.), *Edward Elgar: Letters of a Lifetime* (OUP, 1990)

Nice, David, *Edward Elgar: An Essential Guide to his Life & Works* (Classic fM Lifelines, 1996)

Quennell, Marjorie & C. H. B., *A History of Everyday Things in England*, Volume III (Batsford, 1933)

Pipe, Lucy (née Elgar), 'Reflections' (unpublished MS, Worcester County Record Office)

Redwood, Christopher (ed.), *An Elgar Companion* (Sequoia Publishing, 1982)

Reed, W. H., *Elgar* (J. M. Dent & Sons, 1939)

Sheehy, Kieron & Andrew Holliman (ed.), *Education & New Technologies*, (Routledge, 2018)

Simmons, K. E. L. & Marion, *The Elgars of Worcester* (The Elgar Society, 1984)

Simmons, K. E. L. & Marion, *A Walk Around Elgar's Worcester* (*Elgar Society Journal*, May & September 1985, & January 1986)

Smith, Richard, *Elgar in America* (Elgar Editions, 2005)

Steinbach, Susie, *Understanding the Victorians: Politics, Culture & Society in Nineteenth-Century Britain* (Routledge, 2017)

Sutton, Peter, *Piers Plowman, A Modern Verse Translation* (McFarland & Company Inc, 2014)

Trease, Geoffrey, *Edward Elgar, Maker of Music* (Macmillan & Co., 1959)

Trevelyan, G. M., *English Social History* (Longmans, 1944)

Trott, Michael, *Elgar's Remarkable Mother* (article in *Elgar Society Journal*, March 2004)

Young, Percy M., *Elgar, O.M.* (Collins, 1955)*

Young, Percy M., *Alice Elgar: Enigma of a Victorian Lady* (Dennis Dobson, 1978)

16.
Notes

1. Greenings & Apperleys
1. Peter Sutton, *Piers Plowman, A Modern Verse Translation*, lines 5 & 6.
2. Percy M. Young, *Elgar, O.M.*, p.81, from a letter from Ann to her daughter Pollie, dated 11 December 1898.
3. Zechariah Greening was a younger brother of Joseph Greening's father, William Greening. See Michael Greening, *A Family Story: The Greenings & Some of their Relatives*, p.37.
4. Percy M. Young, *Elgar, O.M.*, footnote on p.20.
5. Marjorie & C. H. B. Quennell, *A History of Everyday Things in England*, volume III, p.136ff.

2. Ann's Childhood in Herefordshire, 1822-c.1840
1. Walter Besant, *The Art of Fiction* (pamphlet), p.6.

3. Ann's Youth & Early Adulthood, c.1840-1848
1. Percy M. Young, *Elgar, O.M.*, p.20.
2. K. E. L. & Marion Simmons, *A Walk Round the Elgars' Worcester* (Part II) (article in *Elgar Society Journal*, September 1985, pp.20-21).
3. *Nucketts Farm* has been identified by Cora Weaver, based upon William Elgar's 1845 map showing the route from Worcester.
4. Percy M. Young, *Elgar, O.M.*, footnote 1 on p.22.
5. Basil Maine, *Elgar: His Life & Works*, Book 1, p.4.
6. *Ibid.*, p.3.
7. Jerrold Northrop Moore, *Edward Elgar, A Creative Life*, p.4.
8. Hubert Leicester (*Notes on Catholic Worcester*, p.33) writes: 'It was to this seemingly secure tradition that the Protestant William Henry Elgar succeeded in 1843 …' However, Percy Young (*Elgar O.M.*, footnote on p.24) and Fr Brian Doolan (*St George's, Worcester, 1599-1999*) quote 1842. Jerrold Northrop Moore (*Edward Elgar, A Creative Life*, p.4) gives 1846, quoting Carice Elgar Blake, MS notes of conversation with Hubert Leicester in 1935. The authors are inclined to believe Percy Young and Fr Brian Doolan: William Elgar became organist at St George's in 1842.

9. Basil Maine, *Elgar: His Life & Works*, Book 1, p.3.
10. Percy M. Young, *Elgar, O.M.*, p.32.
11. *Ibid.*, p.21.
12. *Ibid.*, p.23, and family tree published by the Elgar Society, London Branch, based upon research by Richard C. Powell and Brian Dolan.
13. *Ibid.*, p.32.

4. Marriage & Family Life, 1848-1863
1. Quoted in Percy M. Young, *Elgar, O.M.*, p.24.
2. MS note of Philip Leicester of his father Hubert's conversation with Fr Driscoll, S. J., 28 November 1909, and quoted by Jerrold Northrop Moore in *Edward Elgar, A Creative Life*, p.17.
3. Jerrold Northrop Moore, *Spirit of England: Edward Elgar in his World*, p.6.
4. Basil Maine, *Elgar: His Life & Works*, Book 1, p.4.
5. Aria from Verdi's *La Traviata*.
6. Felicia Hemans, 1793–1835, poet.
7. Matilda Knott is recorded at 10 High Street in the census from 1871 to 1901, but Ned Spiers makes no appearance (he probably lived elsewhere with his wife).
8. Jerrold Northrop Moore, *Edward Elgar, A Creative Life*, p.17.

5. Life at 10 High Street, 1863-1878 (first 15 years)
1. Quoted in Jerrold Northrop Moore, *Edward Elgar, A Creative Life*, p.22.
2. Jerrold Northrop Moore, *Edward Elgar, A Creative Life*, p.27.
3. *Ibid.*, p.22.
4. *Ibid.*, p.30.
5. *Ibid.*, p.21.
6. *Ibid.*, p.28.
7. Newspaper cutting quoted by Jerrold Northrop Moore in *Edward Elgar: A Creative Life*, p. 43.
8. Jerrold Northrop Moore, *Edward Elgar, A Creative Life*, p.93.
9. *Ibid.*, p.52.
10. *Ibid.*, p.38.
11. *Ibid.*, p.56.
12. *Ibid.*, p.60.
13. *The Dungeon.*
14. Jerrold Northrop Moore, *Spirit of England: Edward Elgar in his World*, p.100.

16. Notes

6. Later Years in Worcester, 1878-1902
1. Percy M. Young, *Elgar, O.M.*, p.64.
2. Jerrold Northrop Moore, *Edward Elgar, A Creative Life*, p.86.
3. Jerrold Northrop Moore (ed.), *Letters of a Lifetime*, p.52.
4. Lecture given by Professor John T. Hamilton at the Elgar Birthplace Museum in January 2018 on 'Cross against Corselet: Elgar, Longfellow, and *The Saga of King Olaf*'.
5. Jerrold Northrop Moore (ed.), *Letters of a Lifetime*, p.385.
6. Kevin Allen, *Elgar in Love*, p.71.
7. Percy M. Young, *Elgar, O.M.*, p.81.
8. Told by the friend's daughter to biographer Jerrold Northrop Moore and quoted in his *Edward Elgar, A Creative Life*, p.218.
9. Richard Smith, *Elgar in America*, p.176.
10. *Ibid.*, p.178.
11. Michael Kennedy, *Portrait of Elgar*, p.139.
12. Rosa Burley & Frank C. Carruthers, *Edward Elgar, the Record of a Friendship*, p.161.
13. The cause of Ann's death was given by a Dr Cavenagh as 'Fatty Heart (uncertain), Ascites, Asthenia'. The addition of the word 'uncertain' is curious. Fatty heart refers to fat surrounding the heart, ascites is the accumulation of fluid in the abdomen, and asthenia is physical weakness. Broadly speaking, the cause of death was heart failure.
14. The cause of William's death was given by a Dr Seymour (?) as 'Senility, Circulatory failure' (heart failure).
15. Jerrold Northrop Moore, *Edward Elgar, A Creative Life*, p.374.

7. Ann's Influence on Edward
1. R. J. Buckley, *Sir Edward Elgar*, p.5.
2. Diana McVeagh, *Elgar the Music Maker*, p.84.
3. David Nice, *Edward Elgar: An Essential Guide to his Life & Works*, p.11.
4. *Ibid.*, p.35f.
5. Michael Kennedy, *Portrait of Elgar*, second edition, p.140f.
6. Percy M. Young, *Elgar, O.M.*, p.28.
7. *Ibid.*, p.122.
8. Michael De-la-Noy, *Elgar the Man*, p.20.
9. *Ibid.*, p.27.
10. Jerrold Northrop Moore (ed.), *Letters of a Lifetime*, p.487.
11. W. H. Reed, *Elgar*, p.3.
12. E. Wulstan Atkins, *The Elgar-Atkins Friendship*, p.433.

13. Jerrold Northrop Moore, *Edward Elgar, A Creative Life*, p.18.
14. *Ibid.*, p.6.
15. *Ibid.*, p.546 (quotation from *The Star*).
16. Kieron Sheehy & Andrew Holliman (ed.), *Education & New Technologies*, p.36.
17. Jerrold Northrop Moore, *Edward Elgar, A Creative Life*, p.465.

9. Ann's Scrapbooks
1. Geoffrey Trease, *Edward Elgar, Maker of Music* (Macmillan & Co., 1959).

10. 'Worcester Papers'
1. Hubert A. Leicester, *Forgotten Worcester*, p.9.
2. Percy M. Young, *Elgar, O.M.*, p.25.

12. Concern for Schooling in the Pre-Victorian Period
1. G. M. Trevelyan, *English Social History*, pp.552, 553.

13. The American Connection – Nineteenth-century Emigration
1. Michael Greening, *A Family Story: The Greenings & Some of their Relatives*, p.56.

Appendix
Extracts from 'Worcester Papers'

'Worcester Papers' No.1 Saturday August 14, 1852:

CAPITAL PUNISHMENT

'Worcester Papers' were regular, fairly extensive reports, written around 1852 by William and Ann Elgar to send to William's brother Tom in exchange for a similar 'Dover News'. They show a keen interest in the world around them and original thought.

See Illust. 47 for a facsimile of the title page. Ann's use of English succumbs to the prolixity of her times, so her text that follows has been judiciously redacted to facilitate the reader's understanding of what she has to say. And Ann has lots to say:

> *I think if ever there was a convenient season for discussing the merits or demerits of Capital Punishment, that time is ... the present time ... I need not ... mention my allusion to the case of Mary Robins, the woman who was sentenced to be hanged for the murder of her child ... but ... thanks to the ... generosity of a few persevering individuals, we are to be spared that loathsome and heart-rending spectacle, although ... announced in our Assize Hall to take place in front of the County Gaol. I hope the reader will not imagine I am about to advocate the continuance of crime in any shape. I admit murder to be the most horrible and distressing of crimes, and far too enormous to pass over without subjecting the offender to a very severe punishment, and maintain that the guilty wretch should be allowed to suffer in such a manner that the example should be an every-day one, and not the lesson of an hour. Let the murderer go forth, Cain-like, with a mark set upon him ...*
>
> *It appears to me to be the opinion of every one ... that the main uses of capital punishment are to make of the offender an example, so that the people may take warning and reflect upon the consequences of such a crime ... and by doing so prevent the recurrence of the like again. But we have seen that it has not had the desired effect ... it never can have! ... we must have recourse not to the mere working of the machinery but to the power that puts this machinery in motion; we must look not only to the cut-throat business of the deed, but to*

47. Front page of 'Worcester Papers', 14 August 1852.

Appendix

the relationship the mind of the man bears in accordance to the actual performance of the act. I am ... of the opinion that a being possessed of the organs of "Benevolence" would never ... commit a murder; and ... that one possessed of the organs of "Distinctiveness" would not ... kill a fly. Now, according to the laws of Nature, the greater the intellectual and moral qualities of a man are, the greater propensity will he have for acting nobly and consistently with respect to the laws of civilization. On the contrary, the less he possesses of these faculties, the greater his inclination will be to do things contrary to the rules of the social system of existence ... I will further suppose there are some ... human beings who possess these qualities in either extreme, the one ... to be purely moral – the other with such a mind as will prompt him to commit sins of the blackest dye with the utmost ease ... it will be just as impossible for the one to go through the course of his existence without committing some vile acts of immorality as it would be for the other to deviate ... from the paths of virtue.

... how it is that a savage takes his neighbour to a fire and roasts him alive, and after which sits down in perfect tranquillity with his guests and commences eating him? ... he is conscious ... only... that his victim must be in a state of agonizing torment, and I question much whether in one half of the murders committed in this country the offender is more concerned about the soul of his victim than the untutored barbarian ... But the most striking proof of their natural similarity will be at once discovered by observing the peculiar cast of the cranium ... those persons who commit notorious deeds, or offend largely against the laws of civilization, possess less of these good qualities in proportion to the enormity of their crimes. Therefore ... I hold it unjust to take the life of a fellow creature for the wrongs he has done through acting in accordance to the impulses of his nature, as it is well known in these cases that there must be a lamentable deficiency of sound sense and a total lack of discrimination between good and evil ... I ... argue that the man who commits murder imagines he has done no wrong ... but ... the man who lacks the organs of 'firmness' and 'benevolence' is most sure to follow the impulse of his uncontrollable nature and sees not his error until too late. From this I argue that the hanging of one half of the population of this world for the like offence would deter the remaining portion from committing similar deeds of violence – supposing they were alike in possession of the animal faculties I have spoken of.

In perusing an Article on the subject ... I found the following paragraph, which ... has ... strengthened my opinion on the matter in believing it to proceed from the pen of a very clever writer ... : "Men have confessed to the committing of murder under impulses which they could not account for, but which they were equally unable to restrain." This appears to be in perfect coincidence with what I have been endeavouring to explain ...

It is well known that the establishment of the law enforcing Death by Strangulation for offending against certain statutes of the land (such as murder, house-breaking, horse-stealing, sheep-stealing, forgery, etc., etc.) is of a very remote date, and was ... adopted at a period when little distinction could be found between the learned and ignorant, when the bare idea of a phrenological system of our parts would have been considered as something relating to Demonology and Witchcraft; but I say it is strange that in such times as the present (that) the minds of the community should be ... imposed upon as to allow the death of a fellow-creature to take place on a gallows ... It is a horrible reflection ... and I can find no ... justification in any of the blessed doctrines set forth for our example to act in the manner the law allows ... It is right that every precaution should be taken for the safety of our lands, our houses, our goods, ... our children and ourselves, but let us adopt such measures as really will ... be the means of avoiding such evils. Let us act in such a manner that every one of us may actually profit by the example set forth, instead of arousing our indignation and creating within us a disgust for the established law as is universally felt with respect to Capital Punishment. We all are aware that it is no punishment for the offender – neither does it offer any compensation to the injured party – in fact it does no ... good whatever; and further, if we, as we profess ... to be, are Christians, is there not something truly unreasonable in our actions by deviating ... from the example set us by our Great Master – who, even in the agonizing torments of death, then spoke of his murderers 'Father, forgive them, for they know what they do'?

'Worcester Papers' No.4 Saturday September 4th, 1852:

THE SANITARY QUESTION!!

'Worcester Papers' No.4 deals with the inadequate provision for public sanitation in Worcester.

G. M. Trevelyan sets the scene nationally in *English Social History*:

The new urban conditions, under which so large a proportion of the English people were already living in 1851, began at length to attract attention and demand a remedy. The old life of the open countryside, blown through by the airs of heaven, needed, or was thought to need, less control of housing and sanitation: bad as rural cottages were, the death-rate was lower in the country than in the town.

48. Front page of 'Worcester Papers', 4 September 1852.

The 1848 Public Health Act was the first step to improve public health in England and Wales. It established a Central Board of Health, whose job it was to improve sanitation and living standards in towns. The social reformer Sir Edwin Chadwick, K.C.B. (1800-1890), played an important role in its creation. Joseph Hume, F.R.S. (1777-1855), was a Scottish doctor and Radical M.P. who joined with others to help improve public sanitation as well as the general condition of the working classes, establishing schools for them and forming savings banks.

The following is a pertinent extract from Hansard.

> *Complaints as to the proceedings of the General Board of Health were made by Portsmouth, Dorking, Bromyard, Worcester, Salford, and Brighton. In some cases the local boards repudiated the interference of the General Board ... With regard to Worcester, the mayor and corporation of that city had sent a petition to that House under the corporate seal, and their case was certainly one which required much attention. In fact, the city of Worcester seemed to have been dealt with in a most extraordinary manner. They stated in their petition that the Public Health Act allowed the local board to make bylaws, which were not however to be enforced until approved of by the Secretary of State; and it turned out that these people having made some by-laws according to the Act, and sent them up for the approval of the Secretary of State, that right hon. Gentleman finding himself in the immediate neighbourhood of the Board of Health, handed the by-laws over to them, and received for answer, "By no means agree to them." The petition also stated that the calculation made by the superintendent inspector was based upon the number of deaths that took place in seven years, being twenty-three in a thousand, and that in order to have a good case when he returned to Richmond-terrace, instead of taking the sanitary report for Worcester for the last seven years, he went back to the previous seven years to show that the city came within the provisions of the Act. It appeared further that there was a gaol, a 1743 infirmary, and a tolerably large union-house at Worcester, and that all these institutions were included in the scale upon which the inspector made his calculation for the district. The consequence was, that the mayor and corporation, and the inhabitants, were opposed to the interference of the General Board of Health, and that the business of the city was now at a standstill for want of the necessary by-laws.*

Here is Ann's (redacted) article (see Illust. 48 for a facsimile of the title page):

Appendix

THE SANITARY QUESTION!!

"Although Health is not acclaimed by economists among the elements of national wealth, it is emphatically true that no nation can be prosperous without a healthy population."

… we do intend to lay before our readers a few remarks on the great all-important topic which has lately called forth so much discussion in this city especially. We allude to that of Sanitary Reform! Surely, if the time has arrived when the public authorities of the United Kingdom have just begun to consider the comforts of the poorer classes – when at last they have condescended to stoop a little by way of adding to their comfort – in the shape of Popular Education, Cheap Food, and Clothing and other additional comforts, then, certainly, we can but expect, nay demand … a system of Drainage, Sewerage, so as will enable them to enjoy the greatest boon Heaven has bestowed upon us – Health! designated by one of the most practical of our living writers "the greatest of temporal blessings in the poor man's capital and stock in trade." (Ann refers to the *Sermon on the Poor Man's Contentment* by Jonathan Swift.)

We cannot conceive any greater comfort that can be attached to a man's personal wants than that of a wholesome neat little cottage well ventilated and drained with a plentiful supply of pure water. And we imagine that if more of this comfort were to be found amongst the dwellings of the labouring classes there would be less occasion for … the man of physic. Damp, badly-drained houses are certain to be the abode of the most pernicious of diseases – ague, fever, cholera, etc.; and we say that if a man is conscious of the injury he is causing, in the undermining of his children's constitutions and the destroying of his own, by remaining in such a dwelling, he is much to blame, and I question whether that man would not be justified … in making known his grievances and oppressions and in arousing his neighbours to take an active part with him to … to remove all such nuisances from out of their way. There are no enjoyments without health, no matter what we may be blessed with in the shape of domestic comforts, and it is of no avail without the blessings of Health, and verily that man must be a demon, who for a consideration of a paltry portion of his income would attempt to deny to his fellow creatures … the necessary means for the promotion of health, for the preservation of that which links together body and soul – for health is life itself. And we are given to understand, that there are some of this class of people who are now actively exerting themselves to prevent … the necessary steps being taken for the carrying out of the object of the "Health of Towns Act" in the city of Worcester.

Can it be possible? and for what purpose are they acting thus? will naturally be asked. We cannot tell, but … probably it is a natural feeling of indignation at the monstrous idea of a poor labouring class of people wishing to live … in a wholesome state! but more likely because the introduction of such a system of Sanitary reform in this city would entail upon them … a little further expenditure of their income. Oh, no! it cannot be – we really cannot imagine that anything civilized could be so shamefully void of common humanity …

We are certain of this, that … what tends to no harm must tend to some good.

We feel bound … to make an extract from an able article on this subject. In fact, we like the idea of contrasting the opinions of others with our own on such important subjects – it serves to convince, as well as strengthen our ideas, on many occasions. Speaking of the purity of air as being the essential requisite for health, the author proceeds:

"Tanks and collections of water of every kind are dangerous beneath or near a house, because unless the contents be constantly in a state of change, which is rarely the case, their tendency is to send up exhalations of a noxious kind. A few years ago, the eldest son of an English nobleman … died of a fever which was traced to the opening of an old reservoir of water underneath the country-house in which he dwelt."

It is astonishing when we reflect on the utter carelessness with which we are apt to treat these matters which are of the utmost consequence. Were a certain sum of money to be expended upon such persons as would undertake to carry our most Gracious Queen on their backs for few miles, I warrant few hundreds would be found eager to commence the task. We hold it to be one of the first duties of the Legislative Assembly to provide for the comforts of the labouring portion of the community, and yet it would seem that every new Act is in some way tantamount to a new oppression. And now that there is available for all an Act for the especial benefit of those we would see more in accordance with the spirit of the times, there are many who would wrench even that from their hand. "I do believe," said Mr Hume in a late speech in the House of Commons, "we want the balance restored, and the people's voice heard …" And were this done there are many … new grievances, new wants yet to come to light. It is true we have Education on an extensive scale, and we have Religious Meals too, for all classes and at a cheap rate. We have also cheap food and clothing – and many other things – but we must have more than this, we must have … health to enjoy it – we must have less distinction between the upper classes and the lower classes – more of that spirit of kindness one towards another which is essential to the happiness and contentment of every degree of station in this life … and more of that humility and meekness shown to the labouring portion of the community which is in the power of the wealthy to bestow – we must have more hearty wishes, more encouragement, and more respect given to those who mainly and solely constitute the foundation of this great empire. The lord must not be greater than his servant in this state than in a future one – for we know that … even the Great Master of all is no respecter of persons. And before that … temperament of fellow feeling can pervade the breast of the humbler individual, it must first show itself in the actions of those whom we have always been taught to look up to with the greatest reverence and submission. Before the master claims from his menial a ready compliance with his wishes, let him first take the precaution to render some important service, some substantial benefit, thus proving by such actions that it is equally as pleasing and practicable for the one to bow as well as the other – for we shall all one time have to bow in token of great submission.

In conclusion, if a real and lasting benefit can be bestowed upon us from a mere trifling outlay of capital we pray that no time may be lost in granting this boon to everyone that stands in need, and without further parley, seeing how necessary it is, but the full operation of the Sanitary Measures be adopted to the good City of Worcester.

'Worcester Papers' No.5 Saturday September 11th, 1852:

THE DELUGE OF 1852
Here is Ann's (redacted) article:

There are certain periods of our existence when we are apt to grow careless and inattentive to our first great duties, and more especially at such times when, by a more than ordinary influx of success, we become 'dignified and raised rather above our stations in life'. We certainly must be perfectly conscious that we are solely indebted to our Great Power for all the good and inestimable blessings we receive – yet still, as we have clearly observed, there seems to pervade in most of us a gross negligence of the all-important obligations which we owe to our Benefactor. Were a … person to bestow upon … us unexpectedly a large sum of money, in the shape of a present, we should repay him with thousands of thanks – respect him – may almost reverence him for his … liberality. But on the other hand, if blessed with continued good health, and strength, and happiness at home and abroad, and … securely freed from all the besetting evils which we are continually subject to, scarcely a thought of gratitude or an earnest word of thankfulness is offered to the benevolent, all-merciful Creator in return.

We have lately been visited by one of the most awful tempests that has ever occurred in the county of Worcestershire, within the recollection of the oldest inhabitant. The havoc created has been of the most harrowing description imaginable and everywhere ... is one saddening and lamentable wreck of property. But the most fearful loss of all perhaps may be recorded, the life of a fellow creature – a poor aged woman, who was suddenly swept from her lonely tenement and borne down the rushing torrent to another world! On ruminating the other day over the sorrowful results of this appalling calamity, we were led into a train of thought which continued occupying our attention ... for some moments. Whilst we were speculating on the goodness of God in thus withholding his anger from us that have escaped destruction, we were suddenly flashed with the conviction of our utter worthlessness, and our carelessness in remaining disobedient to Him and His commands, and wondered how we possibly could escape his vengeance, seeing how mighty and instantaneous His power. But the most impressive portion of our reflections ... was the manner in which we ought for the future to act for the mercies bestowed in protecting us from the awful fury of that never to be forgotten night, and a night "unequalled in appalling attributes by anything within living memory".

There is a very important lesson to be learnt from this event. Beginning with those creatures ... who have not the least idea of the boundless power of the Deity, the most ignorant of all mankind, they have now had a demonstration which will never be erased from their minds of the stupendous acts which can be performed by the hand of Him if He wills to do it. The most sceptic also will surely never look around again and say "I must have further proof: these are concerned with the combined agency of the natural order of things – the result of the opposition of the organic laws of Nature – in fact there cannot be one who has witnessed anything of the kind who can remain in doubt of the infinite power of God. Seeing then how soon we might be called to render an account of our actions before Him, let us all take example from the calling of the unfortunate woman, and begin to clothe ourselves with humility and meekness and show by our behaviour how deeply sensible we feel of the great duty we owe to Him. We are as children in the hands of the giant – we know not how soon the hand that guarded us but yesterday may crush us into atoms.

Index

Adelaide, Dowager Queen, 32
Allen, William, 42, 58
Apperl(e)y, Esther (mother); see Greening

Broadheath, Worcestershire, 39-41, 54
Buck, Dr Charles, 58, 73
Buckler, John Chessell, 40

Caractacus, 82
Claines, 14, 26, 30
Cobbett, William, 14
College Precincts, Worcester, 37, 45, 54
Colwall, Herefordshire, 3, 82, 116

Dream of Gerontius, 85-87
Dudley, Lord, 32

Edgar Street, Worcester, 43, 54
Elgar, Carice Irene (granddaughter), 56, 76
Elgar, Caroline Alice (daughter-in-law), 73, 75, 78, 113
Elgar, Edward William (son), 40, 42, 43, 55-58, 60, 69, 72, 73, 75, 76, 78, 79, 82, 83, 85, 86, 88, 95, 101, 119
Elgar, Francis Thomas ('Frank') (son), 45, 63, 70
Elgar, Frederick Joseph ('Joe') (son), 43, 56, 86
Elgar, Helen Agnes ('Dot') (daughter), 46, 63, 76, 102

Elgar, Henry (brother-in-law), 35, 45, 75
Elgar, Henry John ('Harry') (son), 37, 46, 55, 86
Elgar, Lucy Ann (daughter); see Pipe
Elgar, Susanna Mary ('Pollie') (daughter), see Grafton
Elgar, Susanna (sister-in-law), 35, 45
Elgar, Thomas ('Tom') (brother-in-law), 34
Elgar, William Henry (husband), 40, 42, 43, 55-58, 60, 69, 72, 73, 75, 76, 78, 79, 82, 83, 85, 86, 88, 95, 101, 119
Elgar Brothers (music shop), 45, 46, 52, 55
Elmore, Gloucestershire, 3
Elton-by-Newnham, Gloucestershire, 6
Enigma Variations, 82

The Firs (Elgar Birthplace), 40, 69, 104
Forest of Dean, 3, 21

Grafton, Susanna Mary ('Pollie') (daughter), 40, 46, 60, 63, 70, 73, 75
Grafton, William ('Will') (son-in-law), 70, 73
Greening, Charles (nephew), 70, 83, 85, 127
Greening, Esther (mother), 6, 14, 21, 26

Greening, Elizabeth (sister); see Simmonds
Greening, Joseph (father), 3, 14, 21, 26
Greening, John (brother), 21, 26, 36, 70, 83, 127, 130

Handley, 14, 26
Hardy, Thomas, 97
High Street, Worcester, 46, 54, 55, 76
Hope Mansell, 13, 21

Islington, 36

King Olaf, 79-81
Knott, Matilda ('Kit'), 43, 55

Leicester, Hubert, 39, 45, 46, 56, 57, 101, 119
Leicester, John, 42, 43
Leicester, William, 43, 45
Littleton House, 58
Longfellow, 64-66, 80

More, Hannah, 14, 23, 124

Nucketts Farm (Blossom Farm), 26, 30, 32

Old Hills, 67, 68

Pipe, Charles ('Charlie') (son-in-law), 70, 73, 101
Pipe, Lucy Ann (daughter), 24, 34, 37, 40, 42, 46, 55, 60, 69, 70, 73, 101, 105
Pontshill, Herefordshire, 21

Reeve, Francis, 58

St George's Roman Catholic Church, Worcester, 34, 37, 54
The Shades Tavern, 26, 32, 45
Scrapbooks, 108, 113
Shakespeare, William, ix, 117
Simmonds, Elizabeth (sister), 21, 26, 32, 45, 127
Simmons, Francis (brother-in-law), 26
Spetchley Park, 58, 69
Spiers, Ned, 43, 56
Strauss, Richard, 85, 93

Wagner, Richard, 81, 82
Waterworth, Fr, 116
Weston-under-Penyard, 14, 21
Westbury-on-Severn, 14, 103
Walsh, Caroline, 50, 58, 125
Weaver, Helen, 73
Witley Court, 32, 41
Worcester, 26, 30, 37, 43, 46, 52-54, 70
'Worcester Papers', 32, 40, 57, 67, 118, 139